Latin America and the World Recession

The international debt crisis which erupted in 1982 raised a host of questions: about the ability of the international financial system to survive it, and about the future viability of the development models followed until then by Latin American countries. Today the debt problem is far from being resolved. Instead it has been pushed forward: reschedulings have become more common; repayments of principal have been postponed; and bankers have been forced to open new lines of credit for debtors to pay interest on old loans. The pressing questions now are how much will the debtor countries have to repay, when, and who will suffer most from the costs of repayment. Debtor countries face many years of decreasing standards of living; the industrial nations face growing unemployment if they are unable to export to the developing countries. On the other hand, if the governments of the industrialized countries decide to bail out the debtor nations, it will be their taxpayers who will bear the brunt of the crisis.

There has been no shortage of commentary on the debt crisis in Latin America, but it has tended to focus on the problem's immediate features. The aim of this collection of essays by American, British and Latin American scholars is to provide the political and economic background. It examines the causes that led many Latin American countries to contract huge debts, and the effect of world recession on their ability to pay. The internal causes are examined by means of detailed case studies of Brazil, Mexico, Chile, Venezuela and the Central American countries. The external factors are dealt with in the context of oil shocks, world recession, growing protectionism, rising interest rates and decline of international commodity prices.

The book provides a comprehensive account of how the debt crisis came about and considers its consequences for the future development of Latin America and its relations with the industrialized world.

Latin America and the World Recession

EDITED BY

ESPERANZA DURÁN

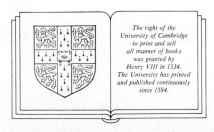

The right of the
University of Cambridge
to print and sell
all manner of books
was granted by
Henry VIII in 1534.
The University has printed
and published continuously
since 1584.

PUBLISHED IN ASSOCIATION WITH

The Royal Institute of International Affairs

Cambridge University Press

CAMBRIDGE

LONDON   NEW YORK   NEW ROCHELLE

MELBOURNE   SYDNEY

Published by the Press Syndicate of the University of Cambridge
The Pitt Building, Trumpington Street, Cambridge CB2 1RP
32 East 57th Street, New York, NY 10022, USA
10 Stamford Road, Oakleigh, Melbourne 3166, Australia

First published 1985

Printed in Great Britain at the University Press, Cambridge

Library of Congress catalogue card number: 84–23834

British Library Cataloguing in Publication Data

Latin America and the world recession.
1. Latin America – Economic conditions – 1945–
I. Durán, Esperanza   II. Royal Institute of
International Affairs
330.98'0038   HC125
ISBN 0 521 30271 4

CE

Contents

Contents

Contributors

VICTOR BULMER-THOMAS, *Lecturer in Economics, Queen Mary College, University of London*

JULIAN M. CHACEL, *Director of Research, Getulio Vargas Foundation*

TIM CONGDON, *Economics Partner, L. Messel & Co.*

ESPERANZA DURÁN, *Research Fellow, Royal Institute of International Affairs*

RAMÓN ESCOVAR SALOM, *Professor of Political Science, Central University of Venezuela*

JONATHAN HAKIM, *Banking Correspondent, 'The Economist'*

LOUISE ORROCK, *Research Student, London School of Economics*

GEORGE PHILIP, *Lecturer in Latin American Politics, Institute of Latin American Studies and the London School of Economics*

GUSTAV RANIS, *Frank Altschul Professor of International Economics, Yale University*

DAVID STEPHEN, *former editor of 'International Affairs'*

JOHN WILLIAMSON, *Senior Fellow, Institute for International Economics, Washington, D.C.*

Preface

In the summer of 1982 the international financial system was shaken by the economic crisis of several deeply indebted Latin American countries whose lack of liquidity and apparent inability to meet their financial obligations compelled the world bankers and international financial institutions thoroughly to re-examine their lending policies. Two years later the implications of the debt crisis have spilt over to the political arena and have involved the leaders of the industrial countries in seeking a solution to what seems to be a long-term problem.

This book derives from the papers presented at a recent study group on Latin America which was held by the Royal Institute of International Affairs at Chatham House. It deals with the development strategies and economic policies of several Latin American countries in the context of the international economic situation. The main questions the essays seek to answer are: what were the causes of the crisis; was it due to the debtor countries' wrong economic policies and overall mismanagement or was it a natural consequence of the world recession and the lending institutions' lack of sound economic forecasting; how can the crisis be overcome?

The introduction places the economic problem in a political context, exploring the relationship between economics and politics in Latin America; it draws parallels and points out contrasts between the different political regimes and the way the political outlook of the governments in power has affected their economic performances.

The first part of the book deals with the topic from a global perspective, examining the Latin American development pattern and the trends in the international economy to explain how the financial crisis came about. This analysis seeks to assess whether the crisis is a short-term debt-service problem or whether, on the contrary, the development models of the major Latin American countries have outlived their usefulness. The macro-economic strategies of several Latin American countries (Argentina, Brazil,

Chile and Colombia) are thus compared among themselves. To give an extra-regional perspective, another type of comparison is carried out: that between the so-called NICs (newly industrializing countries) of Latin America (Brazil, Chile, Colombia and Mexico) and their East Asian counterparts (Hong Kong, Singapore, South Korea and Taiwan).

The second part is a more detailed, country-by-country analysis, which seeks to elucidate how various Latin American economies have fared during the current crisis in the face of their political and economic constraints and decisions. The countries examined are Brazil, Chile, Mexico and Venezuela, as well as Central America. A final essay seeks to identify the main conclusions reached (as well as those questions which have been left open) in the preceding chapters, and to assess the prospects for the future.

I am very grateful to the authors of this volume, who responded promptly and cheerfully to suggestions for revising their papers and to deadlines. I am greatly indebted for valuable advice to Joan Pearce, from whom the idea for this book originated.

July 1984   E.D.

1 The Political Setting: 'Business as Usual' or a New Departure?

DAVID STEPHEN

Elsewhere in this volume, contributions about individual countries or on specific economic topics should help to dispel any notion that the economic problems of the continent are easily diagnosed or, least of all, easily forecast. In the political sphere, however, simplistic ideas – whether about the nature of regimes or of the effect of the international economy on the internal politics of Latin America – continue to flourish. It might, then, be useful to look in general terms at the politics of Latin American countries and to analyse the impact of the world economy on Latin American regimes. The basic theme of this introductory chapter is that analysis of Latin American politics has been bedevilled by false and naive assumptions about the relationship between international economics and internal politics. The world economic recession, and its impact on Latin American politics since the early 1970s, provide ample material for a questioning of those assumptions.

Basically, the usual assumptions are as follows. Many countries in Latin America were formally democratic and had popular governments in the 1960s and 1970s. The Goulart government in Brazil, the Belaúnde government in Peru, the Frei and Allende governments in Chile, and the Radical administration of President Illia in Argentina, as well as the later Peronist government there, were all overthrown by the military after attempting to broaden participation and provide some social and economic advances for the masses. Since the military were the guardians of the interests of the upper classes, and a group whose firm rule would be looked upon with favour by foreign bankers, authoritarian regimes replaced democratic governments in order to preserve the economic *status quo* and keep down wages. The process of incorporation of the masses was thus halted.

These assumptions, although perhaps caricatured here, are, *grosso modo*, shared by a large number of foreign analysts and commentators. A recent

1

volume, which arose from a conference held at the London School of Economics,[1] contains a number of papers arguing in traditional terms about the effect of economic changes in 'metropolitan' countries on the economies of the 'periphery'; the points raised include such ingenious variants of the old theme as the suggestion that, given the problems of 'metropolitan' economies, the attention given by them to the 'periphery' is waning (which explains why metropolitan countries do not nowadays seem to be acting in their own 'interests'), and the unoriginal notion that, as a result of 'debtor power', countries theoretically in thrall to international banks may hold a hitherto unheard-of potential for influence on the world economy.

The pervasive assumption is that Latin American governments, being both peripheral and 'dependent', simply act out a script written for them elsewhere. Unacceptable internal change produces an inevitable response: as Carlos Fortín puts it in the same volume, 'the issue here is the role of increased class polarisation, with the attendant threat to the system leading to an increasingly repressive response'.[2]

This approach begs a large number of purely economic questions, as a lively essay by Carlos Díaz-Alejandro makes clear.[3] Díaz-Alejandro examines the assertion that economic openness in a Latin American country necessarily begets political authoritarianism, and finds the hypothesis wanting. He goes on to suggest that economic performance, at least in the sense of long-term trends, or even macroeconomic performance, was not responsible for the demands for authoritarian rule. What he calls 'unhinged macroeconomic conditions' – including three-digit inflation and unsustainable balance-of-payments deficits – helped to create a chaotic climate which in turn paved the way for the men in uniform. Even given the poor long-term performance of such economies as Chile and Uruguay, there is not automatic correlation leading first to chaotic populism and then to murderous authoritarianism. If there were, says Díaz-Alejandro, India – a long-term low-growth economy – might have followed similar paths; but it has not.

One major factor counselling caution in generalizations about military regimes in Latin America is the variation in their economic policies. The Peruvian junta of General Velasco Alvarado ran a closed economy, with a large measure of state intervention; the Chilean economy combined extreme neo-liberalism in economics with the enforcement, by authoritarian means, of a 'free' labour market; whereas in Argentina, despite the free-market philosophy espoused by General Videla's Economy Minister, José Alfredo Martínez de Hoz, in the mid-1970s, pragmatic considerations, including the need to bargain with the trade union bureaucracy and the size of an entrenched state and military sector with its own protectors or patrons inside the government, meant that many of the 'old' practices persisted.

Yet despite all the economic differences, and differences in time-scale (Brazil 1964, Peru 1968, Argentina 1966 and 1976, Uruguay – with its special variant of Bordaberrización – 1972–3, Chile 1973) the rupture, in terms of political institutions, was everywhere brusque and seemed to herald a new era. For the Argentine political scientist Guillermo O'Donnell[4] the Onganía coup of 1966 in Argentina differed from all previous coups in Argentine history because it represented an attempt to change the political system: the military at that time had no intention of preparing the way for elections but rather to inaugurate a 'bureaucratic-authoritarian' regime. In Brazil a detailed 'doctrine of national security' was worked out by José Alfredo Amaral Gurgel[5] and refined by a soldier-philosopher, General Golbery do Couto e Silva.[6] In Argentina the works of Jorge Atencio provided a justification from the world of geopolitics for the belief that only permanent military rule, or, at the very least, permanent military domination of the political system, could provide the necessary conditions for the preservation of national security and the promotion of economic development. (In Chile, General Pinochet himself had written a text on geopolitics.)

The twin themes of security and development taken up by the military regimes mirrored what had been perceived as the failures of democracy. Security was seen to have been imperilled by the penetration into the body politic of alien elements – usually in the form of alleged communists or subversives or their sympathizers. The perceived softness of the Chilean democratic regime towards the blandishments of the Soviet power bloc, in the form of Cuban penetration of the Chilean revolutionary left, introduced both an international and a security element into the picture, and simultaneously provided a form of legitimation for military intervention. Similarly, the fudging of the lines on the left of the Peronist party in Argentina between those upholding the democratic regime and those actively or subterraneously aiding the cause of the Montoneros or urban guerrillas introduced a legitimizing 'national security' factor into domestic politics.

The stress on endangered national security was present in most of the coups being discussed here, and, again, this was a new element. The instigators of coups habitually claim to be intervening to save democracy or the constitution, or to prevent undemocratic elements from taking over the political system, but the post-1964 coups in Latin America stressed the grave dangers facing the nation from *outside*, publicly at least, rather more than the internal political threats.

3

In Brazil, in the highly developed theories of General Golbery, or in Chile, where military law was used against Marxists on the grounds that Marxists were the ideological servants of an enemy power (the Soviet Union) and therefore 'enemy agents', the concept of national security was taken to great lengths. The nation was being eaten away: only the institution of the military stood between the nation and chaos. The presence of communists among the groups of those held responsible for bringing the nation to such a pass helped in some cases, of course, to legitimize the intervention in the eyes of the world outside. Internal political battles could be given global significance if it could be argued that national security was in danger both from inside and from outside intervention. Amid atmospheres of extreme insecurity the military came in pledged not only to end the insecurity but also to eradicate its causes. 'Democracy' therefore became indefensible: on the contrary, in the Chilean/Argentine/Uruguayan case, democratic institutions had been abused and distorted by rascals, according to the military.

Economic policy as such never figured prominently in the initial statements of the coup-makers. A fourteen-point statement put out by the Chilean Junta shortly after the coup stressed the fact that fundamental rights had been under attack by the Allende administration: it also stressed the 'moral and economic collapse' of Chile, and spoke of 'inflation and the paralysis of trade, industry and agriculture'.[7]

The Junta's own *Declaración de Principios*, published in March 1974, described Chile as a developing country caught up in the cold war, which had chosen one of two antagonistic paths: the Junta had chosen the 'Christian concept' of man, putting him above the state and defining him as a 'spiritual being'. A pro-Junta account of the coup attacked the minister responsible for the economic policy of the Allende government, Pedro Vuskovic, as someone whose aim had been 'the destruction of the capitalist economy in order to build a "new order" on its ruins'. In the 1976 coup of General Videla in Argentina, the elimination of subversion had figured with the eradication of corruption as the major objectives of the 'process of national reconstruction'. General Golbery's theories in Brazil stressed the need for economic development: the nation should take control of the major areas of the economy in order to establish national development goals. The post-coup governments in Brazil, Argentina and Chile were all in theory committed to the free-market economy, though (as chapters elsewhere in this volume make clear) with varying degrees of rigour in their adherence to the free-market in practice.

In economics, as in politics, the conviction was that something had broken down. Clientelism, corrupt trade unionism, privileges for officials and elected representatives, distortions in the economy by economic demagogy: the general feeling was that matters were out of hand. No doubt also intelligence reports about the private lives of senior politicians – and, in particular, their financial affairs – helped to create, among the senior military, the conviction that such people could not be relied upon to defend the nation should a real crisis of national security ensue.

Inflation was 'corroding' the system: there was a pervasive undermining of integrity by corruption. In Chile there was a Marxist 'cancer' to be 'extirpated' or extinguished by the use of 'antibodies' (counter-terrorism) if necessary. The metaphors of insecurity proliferated.

But what was it that had broken down? Despite the pretensions of General Onganía, Argentine democracy did not come to an end for ever in 1966: but what exactly died with Salvador Allende on 11 September 1973? No understanding of the apparent crisis of 'bureaucratic-authoritarian' states today can advance unless we clarify exactly what happened on their enthronement: is an interrupted process being resumed as democratic governments, like that of President Alfonsín in Argentina, are elected to replace the military juntas? Or was there an interruption of the regime, when the military wrought their coups, so that the return of democracy takes place in a new context?

It was pseudo-democracy which came to an end in the military-ruled countries. In Peru, Julio Cotler argues,[8] the coup in 1968 forced through reforms which the elected reformist government had been prevented from carrying out, and acted thus as a guarantor of a stability which might have been in danger had hard-line conservatives stood in the way of the reforms. Congress had opposed some of the measures which Belaúnde thought essential to deal with the country's economic problems: tax reform, industrial and agrarian reform, and a system of economic planning. Because, Cotler argues, the intransigence of Congress and those whose interests it represented threatened social cohesion, the military in effect – though without mobilizing the population and without popular participation – carried out the programme to which the *Acción Popular* government had been pledged. For Cotler the key to understanding the role of the military in the Peruvian case is to be found both in the armed forces' perception that the way to preserve internal security lay with the reformists and in the fact that reforms brought in by the armed forces would be technocratic in character, without any risk that mass mobilization might occur and get out of hand.

Whether these underlying causes advanced by Cotler are satisfying or

5

not, the important point about the Peruvian coup was the conviction that the government had become ineffective. The fear of mass mobilization, whether or not it had any basis in reality (and one suspects that Cotler's attempt to rationalize the position of the armed forces derives from his perception that some circles in his country perceived a 'danger' of mass mobilization, rather than from any independent observation that such an event was probable) illustrates the loss of faith in the democratic process. Whether one views the problem as purely technical (a president locked in battle with Congress) or as deeper and more structural (the oligarchy opposing reformist policies) the fact remains that the political system appeared incapable of moving forward to solve it. It had, in fact, become divorced from the power base which it ought to have had either through its control of economic policy, or because of the authority linked with its office. But the political system ceased to behave as though it controlled events, and appeared to be an irrelevant talking-shop divorced from power.

At first sight the situation in Chile in 1973 seems totally different. There, one is told, the reformist government was opposed by a violent right-wing military regime bent on 'reactionary' economic policies. The Allende administration had embarked on a programme of agrarian reform, income distribution and price control, and had begun an ambitious programme of structural change in the economy. Some of these programmes were undoubtedly effective in incorporating into Chilean society – for the first time – some groups which had until then been virtually excluded from economic or political participation; but these socialist policies also brought other effects in their wake. As the Inter-American Development Bank reported,[9]

In the first nine months of 1973, Chile was plagued by runaway inflation, a reduction in the supply of goods, a widespread black market, a decline in real income, an increasing fiscal deficit in the public sector – including the enterprises of the Area of Social and Mixed Ownership (APSM) – a critical situation in the balance of payments, negative net international reserves and the virtual suspension of external debt-servicing payments.

Politics in Chile in 1973 were highly polarized ideologically, and imported rhetoric – whether the rhetoric of Marxist revolution or of European reaction – flourished: and no doubt some blame for a part of Chile's international financial plight at that time can be laid at the door of those governments and individuals which went out of their way to be as unhelpful as possible to Allende's socialist experiment. But, as in Peru five years earlier, the overwhelming sensation was that matters were not under the control of the elected government. Either, it was thought, extremists had taken charge within the government, or else foreign governments opposed to political and economic freedom were fast gaining in influence. All of the factors reported by the Inter-American Development Bank contributed to an overwhelming sense of chaos and despair. The violent nature of the reaction can be explained by the fact that, in the Chilean case, the internal security aspect of the general sense of chaos took on an international and geopolitical dimension. The armed forces gave legitimacy to their intervention, and endowed it with its special virulence, by linking the internal chaos with sinister external forces in a potent mixture of right-wing nationalism and old-style extreme anti-communism. Whether there ever was any possibility of geopolitical change in Chile is doubtful, given the country's geography and above all the length of its coast and its land frontiers, not to mention its distance from the Soviet Union. There must be few countries whose economy and defence it would be more difficult for the Soviet Union to control. But that hardly matters. The opinion-forming classes in Chile have long believed their country to be European in everything but its geography, and the fear of a Soviet communist take-over was a powerful reality. Conversely, Chile's socialist intellectuals used the language of European revolution, and made much of European socialist concepts of class war.

When asked whether he minded being called 'Excellency', Allende replied, 'I am not just another president, but the first president of a popular, national, revolutionary government which is opening the road to socialism. Moreover, I am not His Excellency the President of the Republic, I am comrade president.'[10] Such statements may, in retrospect, seem trivial and demagogic, but, given the insecurity of the middle classes in Chile under Allende, they serve to accentuate the sense of doom and threat to the established order. Allende's alleged statement, 'I am *not* the President of all Chileans' is still quoted by the middle-class Chileans as one of their late president's more shocking and outrageous statements: discussions were frequently broadcast in which left-wing militants denounced the 'farce' of 'bourgeois legality' and it is clear that, as 1973 drew on, fear and insecurity changed into hatred and panic. Both sides claimed that external forces were intervening: the Allende government claimed that anti-government strikes were backed by the CIA and ITT. The virulent nature of the reaction can thus be explained by the insecurity generated by the actions and inflamed by the political language used under the previous regime. The rhetoric of the 'world's first elected Marxist president' leads inexorably to the repression and the authoritarianism. But the focus of analysis should be the underlying causes of the ending of the democratic regime itself, rather than the fate of

7

the socialist experiment and the personal tragedy of Allende. But did the Allende government have a clear and serious view of how their revolution would proceed? So much of Allende's time seems to have been spent coping with the ultra-left and its pressures that it sometimes appears that more highly disciplined and dogmatic groups had found an ideological vacuum in the administration, and sought to fill it. Politics had become an obsession in itself rather than a question of how the country was to be governed. The sense of chaos and confusion was exacerbated by rhetoric, the heat of which seems to have increased in direct proportion to the inability of the political leaders to find solutions to the country's economic problems. The failure of left-wing propaganda to produce the type of responses which the left had predicted caused bitterness, and therefore set the scene for the creation of right-wing or 'imperialist' scapegoats to intervene and upset the process: and it also encouraged and inflamed the rhetoric of counter-revolution. Scapegoats on both sides helped to disguise the fact that the political system could not, apparently, produce the goods which those who worked within it had promised. The political system became detached from the levers of real power, particularly in the economic sphere, as money moved abroad and international bankers and the United States administration began their boycott of the socialist economy. The rhetoric increased, producing not merely what it had promised, but social collapse. The fault was not solely that of the socialists, but of a political system which had grown apart from the society which it sought to serve.

The Argentine coup of 1976 took place in similar structural conditions. Following the death in 1974 of President Perón, Argentina had been ruled by his widow, Isabel Martínez de Perón, and while populist rhetoric had continued – consonant with Peronism's portrayal of itself as the embodiment of Argentine national and working-class aspirations – the reality was rather different. Power passed to a right-wing clique who held influence over the president, and economic policies became more and more conservative, while repression of the revolutionary Montonero group within the Peronist party was stepped up. The scenario was therefore one of increasing bitterness and alienation among the government's supporters, bewilderment and insecurity among the middle classes and hostility among businessmen and bankers who failed to see that the government was in fact carrying out the type of policies which they had advocated. As in the Chilean case, there was a divorce between the language of politics and what happened (or failed to happen): and important sectors of the population therefore supported the military coup.

The government of Isabel Perón and of her astrologer/adviser José López

Rega was, then, quite different in outlook from that of Allende in Chile. It was in no way socialist and represented no threat to 'bourgeois' interests. Indeed, the Peronist government, certainly following the death of President Perón in 1974 and the ascent of López Rega and his clique, was right-wing both in its general economic outlook and in its attitude towards internal security. There were no plans, even in blueprint, for massive extensions of public ownership or massive agrarian reform: and although there was a shift, in external trade policy, towards large barter deals with Soviet bloc countries, no plausible case could be made out that Argentina was about to undergo a geopolitical transformation. There was, however, a pervasive sense of chaos amid what Díaz-Alejandro would call 'unhinged macro-economic conditions',[11] and there was a rise in the level of rhetoric, particularly about revolution, as guerrilla groups, with a penetration deep inside the official Peronist party, called for the overthrow of the discredited, 'rotten', system. With galloping inflation, the sense of impending collapse brought the military and their supporters (who were very numerous in early 1976) to the conclusion that a new start was necessary.

Argentine politics have always been more *sui generis* than Chilean politics: the Chileans have always conducted their political discourse in European terms. Virtually every major political party in Chile claims close affinity with one of the European political party 'families'. For all its apparently uniquely Argentine character, Peronism, once defined as working-class-based fascism by Seymour Martin Lipset,[12] was invented by Perón after he had spent a period in Mussolini's Italy.

Uruguay, for its part, was happy to be described, until the collapse of democratic institutions there in the early 1970s, as the 'Switzerland' of Latin America. These imported political models merely complicate the pre-coup picture. Political elites in the Southern Cone – whether of the right, left or centre – have always spoken the political language of Europe, and in particular of Latin Europe. It could even be argued that Latin American political elites have become alienated from their own environment, with political systems which have adopted European models and have become divorced from conditions inside the country. In Chile the Allende government's claim to be the first ever elected 'Marxist' government, has been matched by the belief, widely disseminated abroad by exiles after the 1973 coup, that the Pinochet regime was a world-breaker in brutality and arbitrariness, and by the Pinochet regime's successful recruitment to its cause of neo-liberal economists from North America and Europe anxious to see their views embodied in an economic policy.

Differences in the political histories of the various countries – Peru with

9

its tradition of oligarchic rule, often bolstered by military dictators; Chile with its interrupted democratic record (with the Junta thus represented as a terrible departure from tradition); and Argentina with its almost institutionalized conservative coups – should not blind us to the similarities of what followed. The military regimes, whether 'progressive' like the Peruvian military government under Velasco Alvarado, conservative like the Argentine post-1976 government of General Videla, or right-wing and neo-Franquist like the Pinochet junta, all embarked on conservative economic policies. As other chapters in this volume make clear, all three military juntas seemed well placed, in the world economy that developed after the oil price rise in 1973, to receive dollar loans. They all followed experiments in democracy variously characterized as weak or extremist: all seemed to be formed by people international bankers could deal with.

What is more, in terms of international relations all three juntas were welcomed by the West. True, the Peruvian junta edged its way towards Moscow (and spent some of the hard currency it borrowed on Soviet arms and equipment); and the human rights records in both Argentina and Chile caused the United States, particularly under the Carter administration, to exert various pressures at various times, including arms embargoes. But the recycling of petrodollars to Latin American countries, and particularly to the military-ruled countries, was welcomed by Western governments. For them the recycling operation was a success, and a tribute to the efficacy of Western financial institutions.

But the juntas, and the reaction to them of most Western governments, were based on a mis-diagnosis of the defects of what had gone before. The basic problem did not lie with the policies of the previous regimes, such as socialism in Chile, or the Allende government's attempt to align Chile internationally with the Soviet bloc: it was definitely not a question of a threat from the revolutionary left (the Montoneros in Argentina or the Tupamaros in Uruguay never had significant support in the population, although their terrorist activities caused considerable disruption and were often spectacular). The problem was the inability of political regimes based on competition between political parties and on elections to produce leaders who were themselves capable of working within a democratic framework and of setting the parameters of democratic discourse. As Dr Raúl Alfonsín himself put it in a speech at Castro Barros, Buenos Aires, in July 1982, 'We saw democracy as a competition for votes rather than as a way of life.'[13] Democracy had not delivered the goods, particularly to the poorest sections of the community. Alfonsín clearly saw the military interlude as part and parcel of the old process, and looked to the return to democracy not as a return to unfinished business but as a new start which would have the task of laying the foundations for an enduring democracy. The military period had occurred because of the defects of the previous democratic regime, and so was in a way a continuation of it: what was needed was a deep and meaningful commitment to democracy going far beyond electoral competitions to affect the government and administration and the judicial process as well.

The mis-diagnosis of the problem was radical in its thrust. Since democracy had become undisciplined (and there were many suggestions that democracy was only workable by people of Anglo-Saxon race or traditions) the juntas saw their role as imposing discipline: where demagogy and populism had, it was said, reigned before, the military would reintroduce traditional standards of hard work and personal service. The activities of subversives would be rigorously controlled and infiltration by the rival super-power would be ended. Abroad, the juntas were seen as financially responsible, ending the rule of unreliable politicians who had made deals with trade unions, foreign companies or each other. Massive loans were made because what had been thought to be the defects of Latin American governments had been eradicated.

The obsession with the rhetoric of politics seemed to prevent the emergence of any widespread attempt to discuss and analyse the problem rationally. Changes were fast taking place in the societies of the Southern Cone countries, and economic relations with the United States were very far from being as close as both left and right, from different standpoints, seemed to believe. Society was becoming more 'modern' in the sense that urbanization and industrialization were proceeding apace. But the juntas had set about governing as traditional developing societies countries which were in fact approaching the European norm and in which class-based politics might have been expected to flourish.

The changes in the economies of the Southern Cone countries and Brazil were occurring as the military were taking or consolidating their power. Primary products were declining as a proportion of exports. Between 1970 and 1974 primary products represented an average of 31, 58, and 68 per cent of all exports from Argentina, Brazil and Chile respectively: by 1980 the comparable figures were 25, 35 and 57 per cent respectively.[14] The 1970s saw a rise in the growth of manufactured exports: in terms of penetration of the markets of the industrialized countries, Latin American exports of textiles, clothing, pulp and paper did better in the 1970s than those from East Asia.

The 1970s also saw pronounced changes in the destination of Latin

11

American exports to developing countries, both within Latin America and beyond. To take the example of Argentina: exports to the countries of the European Community (i.e., to those countries at present members of the EEC), the United States, and Latin America accounted for 60 per cent, 9 per cent and 13 per cent during the period 1961–3, but were 33 per cent, 6 per cent and 26 per cent by 1977–9. Imports into Argentina came 27 per cent from the United States, 40 per cent from the EEC, and 13 per cent from the Latin American region in 1961–3, and 19 per cent, 28 per cent, and 23 per cent respectively in 1977–9.[15] In other words, dependence on primary products exported to North America and Europe was decreasing.

The role of the state in the Latin American economies was also changing. According to Inter-American Bank statistics[16] central government revenues and expenditure both increased, not simply in numerical terms, but also as a percentage of total revenue and expenditure. In Chile, central government expenditures rose, as a percentage of total expenditures, from 75 per cent in 1970 to 93 per cent in 1981: in Argentina, central government current transfers and subsidies rose, as a percentage of total expenditures, from 22 per cent in 1970 to 35 per cent in 1980. Some traditional activities of the interventionist state – like nationalizations, and the raising of direct taxation – did not occur, but 'development' figured prominently in the designs of the Brazilian military and, whether by control of the exchange rate or by control of money supply, governments in Chile and Argentina under military rule began to exert a greater measure of control over the economy.

In the Southern Cone itself, the arrival of the juntas coincided with the acute problems caused by the threefold rise in oil prices. Yet countries without appreciable indigenous energy supplies, such as Chile, and those with large and only partially-developed reserves, like Argentina, continued to embark on programmes of economic expansion, stimulated imports while restraining exports by maintaining high currency values against the dollar, and then had recourse, in the late 1970s and early 1980s, to foreign borrowing. Structural adjustment was thus avoided or postponed, while the brunt of such adjustment policies as were introduced fell internally on the most defenceless sectors of the population.

The actual chain of events can therefore be perceived: and the reality is very different from the neo-Marxist caricature. The juntas, far from acting out a script written for them in Wall Street or the City of London, were reacting politically against what they perceived to be the defects of democracy. They reacted against democracy when the defects of the democratic system required regime changes: they reacted against working-class politics as subversive and Marxist because the language and style of the left seemed to be imported from hostile nations, when the language and style of politics in general was in fact imported. But the soldiers chose opposite policies to those which they imagined had brought their countries near to ruin: right-wing where left-wing rhetoric had prevailed before; the free market where private deals and clientelism had seemed to hold sway. But their system, like the democratic system which had preceded it, failed to take into account the relative position in the world economy of the countries ruled. Like the democratic leaders, they persisted in the illusion of sovereignty. The price they paid for their illusion was foreign debt on an unprecedented scale.

NOTES

1 D. Tussie (ed.), *Latin America in the World Economy* (Aldershot, 1983).
2 C. Fortín, 'The Relative Autonomy of the State and Capital Accumulation in Latin America: Some Conceptual Issues', in Tussie, *op cit.*
3 'Open Economy, Closed Polity?', in Tussie, *op. cit.*
4 Guillermo O'Donnell, 'Permanent Crisis and the Failure to Create a Dynamic Regime: Argentina 1955–66', in J. J. Linz and Alfred Stepan (eds.), *The Breakdown of Democratic Regimes: Latin America* (Baltimore and London, 1978).
5 José Alfredo Amaral Gurgel, *Seguranca e Democracia* (Rio de Janeiro, 1975).
6 Golbery do Couto e Silva, *Geopolítica do Brasil* (Rio de Janeiro, 1967).
7 Hernán Millas, *Anatomía de un Fracaso: La Experiencia Socialista Chilena* (Santiago, 1973).
8 Julio Cotler: 'A Structural Historical Approach to the Breakdown of Institutions: Peru', in Linz and Stepan, *op. cit.*
9 Inter-American Development Bank, *Annual Report 1974* (Washington, D.C., 1974).
10 Quoted in Millas, *op. cit.*
11 'Open Economy, Closed Polity?', in Tussie, *op. cit.*
12 S. M. Lipset, *Political Man* (London, 1960).
13 Recording in possession of the author.
14 Inter-American Development Bank, *1982 Report: Economic and Social Progress in Latin America: the External Sector* (Washington, 1982).
15 *Ibid.*
16 *Ibid.*

PART ONE

The Global Perspective

2 Latin America's Financial Crisis: Causes and Cures

JONATHAN HAKIM

When Mexico told its creditors in August 1982 that it could not pay its debts, neither banks nor borrowers nor governments were prepared for the financial crisis that quickly engulfed the rest of Latin America. How did the crisis reach such a pitch with apparently so little warning? Why did borrowers and lenders act as they did, and what were their shares of responsibility? Is the crisis simply a short-term liquidity problem, or does it have deeper roots in the development model of the major Latin American countries? Does the crisis threaten the solvency of individual banks – or even of the banking system as a whole? And will the *ad hoc* measures so far employed to tackle the debt crisis suffice? These are the issues that we try to explore below.

Developments in the 1970s

To understand the present situation we must go back to the beginning of the 1970s. Up to that time international banks were little involved in the business of development finance. They had concentrated their activities in Latin America (as in other parts of the developing world) on three areas: financing international trade through short-term loans; financing investment or working capital of multinational companies established in the countries; and domestic banking activity in those countries where a limited number of international banks had established branches. In exceptional cases some countries received bank loans for balance-of-payments support (often guaranteed by gold) or for projects guaranteed by third parties or by pledging of export contracts. But overall, bank finance accounted for just 7 per cent of the annual capital inflows to Latin America in the 1960s; most of those inflows – 70 per cent – came from official credits and direct foreign investment.

By the end of the 1970s, that situation had been completely reversed, with banks accounting for some 70 per cent of net capital flows. As at end-1983, over three-quarters of Latin America's total outstanding external

17

debt of some $336 billion was owed to private banks. Moreover, as much as 80 per cent of this newly-acquired bank debt was in the form of 'syndicates' – pooled-risk loans shared among many banks carrying floating rates of interest, which adjust in line with market interest rates. As a result, variable-rate debt accounts for between half and three-quarters of the long-term debt of the big Latin American borrowers. That is one of the seeds of the present debt crisis.

The surge in bank lending to Latin America, and to less-developed countries (LDCs) in general, began in 1974–5 after the first oil shock (see Table 2.1). Higher oil prices and the ensuing world recession quadrupled the current-account deficit of non-oil LDCs, not simply because of the higher oil prices and slower-growing export markets, but also because expectations of a continued rise in oil revenues encouraged the net oil exporters, such as Venezuela and Mexico, to increase their expenditures and run bigger current-account deficits financed by borrowing.

Banks were the natural vehicle for recycling the huge financial surpluses accumulated by the OPEC countries. Most of the surplus funds were deposited at short term in the international banks, which in turn were able to establish mechanisms for quick disbursement of loans to the deficit countries with few strings attached – in sharp contrast to the often-tortuous bureaucratic procedures of international agencies such as the World Bank. The new lending was encouraged by the governments of the industrial countries, who were concerned that the OPEC surplus (up from $7 billion in 1973 to $68 billion in 1974) would continue at very high levels because of what they saw as OPEC's limited capacity to absorb imports.

Profitability was also a powerful incentive for the banks to take on this new role. In general the interest-rate margins over cost of funds (the 'spread') paid by developing-country governments were substantially higher than those paid by first-class corporate borrowers – although there were periodic exceptions. The amount of legal and financial work for a loan to a government or government-guaranteed borrower was much less than for a corporation. And as for the risk, the dominant view was, as a number of leading bankers stated publicly, that countries could not go bankrupt whereas corporations could – and do.

On the whole, the recycling after the first oil shock proceeded much more smoothly than even the optimists had dared to expect. The major industrial countries, concerned about the employment effects of higher oil prices, pursued accommodative economic policies, while the surge of bank lending to LDCs meant that finance was available for their growing import bill. World trade continued to grow and commodity prices recovered quickly

Table 2.1 *Latin American debt*

The figures represent total disbursed debt, debt owed by public sector[a], private sector[b], and short-term debt[c], end-year ($ million)

	1975	1979	1980	1981	1982	1983[d]
Argentina						
Total	6,026	19,668	27,065	32,276	36,680	40,718
Public	3,121	8,557	10,187	10,506	16,587	18,590
Private	1,193	5,439	6,593	12,166	12,311	12,353
Short-term	1,712	5,672	10,285	9,604	7,782	9,775
Brazil						
Total	23,344	51,482	64,631	74,051	83,206	91,613
Public	13,751	35,618	39,151	43,829	45,013	54,312
Private	9,593	15,864	16,580	19,622	24,640	24,700
Short-term	NA	NA	8,900	10,600	13,553	12,602
Chile						
Total	4,854	8,484	11,084	15,542	17,153	17,654
Public	3,731	4,812	4,720	4,430	5,171	7,619
Private	536	2,695	4,693	8,123	8,644	8,335
Short-term	587	977	1,671	2,989	3,338	1,700
Colombia						
Total	3,572	5,935	7,310	8,229	10,300	10,500
Public	2,348	3,343	4,048	5,076	6,300	6,701
Private	297	562	925	940	1,005	822
Short-term	927	2,030	2,337	2,213	2,995	2,978
Mexico						
Total	16,900	40,800	52,652	75,496	82,450	86,516
Public	11,540	29,242	33,586	42,642	51,925	67,783
Private	5,022	8,365	7,300	10,200	8,100	8,738
Short-term	338	3,193	11,766	22,654	22,425	9,994
Peru						
Total	4,066	7,116	8,839	8,844	10,356	11,592
Public	3,021	5,932	6,168	5,974	7,125	8,113
Private	230	563	1,372	1,507	1,651	2,304
Short-term	815	621	1,299	1,363	1,580	1,175
Venezuela						
Total	5,700	23,700	27,500	29,300	31,800	32,804
Public	1,262	9,805	10,873	11,352	12,000	12,000
Private	995	2,515	3,853	8,588	13,800	13,810
Short-term	3,443	11,380	12,774	9,360	6,000	6,994

Table 2.1 (*cont*).

	1975	1979	1980	1981	1982	1983[d]
Latin America						
Total	75,393	184,193	229,054	279,697	314,630	336,230
Public	44,956	112,096	126,940	144,791	166,521	204,871
Private	19,340	41,769	46,975	69,668	79,251	80,265
Short-term	11,097	30,328	55,139	65,238	68,588	51,094

[a] Public and private debt with official guarantee and original maturity term greater than one year.
[b] Private debt without official guarantee, maturity of over one year.
[c] Maturity under one year.
[d] Preliminary estimates.
NA = not available.
Source: Inter-American Development Bank.

from the recession; prices of Latin America's non-oil commodity exports rose by 26 per cent in 1976. As a result of this rebound Latin America's real GDP (Gross Domestic Product) growth was sustained at an average annual rate of 4.2 per cent in 1975–7. By 1978 the combination of rapid growth in OPEC imports and a 20 per cent fall in the real price of oil led to the elimination of the OPEC surplus. Part of the benefit accrued to the non-oil developing countries, whose current-account deficits narrowed. Latin America's current-account deficit fell from a peak of nearly 5 per cent of GDP in 1975 to 3.5 per cent two years later.

The LDC borrowers were also helped by declining real interest rates. Defining the real interest rate is somewhat problematic. One common measure is the London inter-bank offered rate (LIBOR) on three-month US dollar deposits less the rate of US inflation, measured by the US GDP deflator. Rising inflation in the United States meant that on this yardstick the real interest rate averaged only 0.5 per cent during 1974–8. But it may be argued that this measure is not the most appropriate, since it fails to reflect the opportunity cost of funds to the borrower. A more relevant index might be LIBOR less the rate of increase in export prices of the non-oil developing countries. On this measure real interest rates were actually negative for much of the period.

The second oil shock

Things did not begin to go seriously wrong, then, until after the second oil shock of 1979. A series of factors, both external and internal, made the environment for Latin American countries much more difficult after this second shock than it had been in 1974–5.

1. *The response of the industralized countries.* Beginning with the British government in October 1979 and followed shortly by the United States, the major industrial countries became convinced that the upward spiral of inflation during successive business cycles had to be brought to an end. But the political difficulties of curbing government spending meant that the burden of fighting inflation was borne almost entirely by restrictive monetary policies, culminating in record high nominal interest rates. Three-month LIBOR jumped from an average of 12 per cent in 1979 to 14.1 per cent in 1980 and to nearly 17 per cent in 1981. With the bulk of Latin America's external debt now at floating rates of interest, this automatically raised debt-servicing charges. The effect was dramatic; interest and profit payments from Latin America practically trebled between 1978 and 1981, with nearly half the increase (around $20 billion) attributable to the rise in nominal interest rates from their 1976–7 average levels. On top of this, amortization payments began to increase as commercial loans contracted in the first half of the 1970s began to mature. Consequently, even without any deterioration in Latin America's current-account deficit, a steep increase in gross borrowing would have been necessary simply to keep the net inflow of capital constant (see Table 2.2).

2. *The length and depth of the recession.* This was underestimated by banks, by borrowers and by governments of industrial countries alike. It resulted in a sharp contraction in the industrial economies (Latin America's main export market) and in international commodity prices – *The Economist's* all-items dollar commodity price index fell from a peak of 236.3 in November 1980 (1975=100) to a low of 143.9 in October 1982. The metals index showed prices, in June 1982, at their lowest levels in real terms for 30 years. This sharp reversal in Latin America's terms of trade brought about a deterioration in the trade balance, from a negligible deficit of $319 million in 1979 to $2.8 billion (22 per cent of visible exports) by 1982. The second effect of the decline in export prices was to send the real implicit interest rate on Latin America's loans (i.e. LIBOR deflated by the rate of increase in export prices) soaring to nearly 20 per cent by 1981–2.

3. *Banks' complacency.* The successful adjustment to the first oil shock and the rarity of losses on loans to governments ('sovereign' loans) encouraged international banks to overestimate the ability of LDCs to continue servicing their debts. The banks went on lending despite the fact that in many countries economic policies were clearly going to result in serious imbalances and unsustainable balance-of-payments positions. The widespread attitude that 'companies may fail but countries do not' overlooked

Table 2.2 *Debt disbursements, debt service and net resource transfers to Latin America ($ million)*

	1976	1977	1978	1979	1980	1981	1982	1983
Gross disbursements	31,387	29,812	52,638	53,326	64,336	72,069	62,421	49,630
Amortization	8,551	11,791	16,913	21,108	19,475	21,426	27,758	27,760
Net disbursements	22,836	18,021	35,725	32,218	44,861	50,643	34,663	21,870
Interest	6,643	7,711	10,870	16,745	21,128	32,527	38,545	39,051
Net transfer	16,193	10,310	24,855	15,473	20,733	18,116	−3,882	−17,181

Source: Inter-American Development Bank.

two important distinctions. First, although domestic loans often incorporate provisions which restrict a firm's overall indebtedness, such provisions are seldom, if ever, included in sovereign loans because they are difficult to enforce. And secondly, while it is true that countries do not go out of business, they are not always able to pay their debts on time.

4. *Failure by borrowing countries to adjust to the new climate.* Partly because they underestimated the severity of the recession, and partly because they continued to have easy access to foreign credit, most Latin American countries did not make the necessary adjustments in their economic policies. There was little incentive to check those longer-term features of Latin American development models which have helped increase external indebtedness – including erratic exchange-rate and interest-rate policies, high-cost industrialization protected by tariff barriers, and subsidized public enterprises subject to little financial discipline.

5. *Build-up of short-term debt.* This was an important feature of the crisis, and accounts for the apparent suddenness with which it broke. By itself, short-term debt need not be a cause for concern, since it is an integral part of international trade. For example, the production and processing of a crop for export is often financed by foreign bank loans which are automatically repaid some months later as the product is exported and payment received. A significant amount of short-term debt (perhaps the equivalent of three to six months of imports) is therefore quite acceptable. However, by early 1982 a number of Latin American countries had borrowed short-term funds far beyond this level (see Table 2.1). Even Brazil, which loudly proclaimed its policy of borrowing only medium-term funds, albeit at the cost of higher spreads, accumulated around $10 billion of short-term debt in the form of inter-bank loans to Brazilian banks.

As market terms became stiffer for Latin American borrowers from early 1980, the countries found they were able to obtain lower interest rates and a larger volume of borrowings from the banks by 'temporarily' borrowing for short terms of one year or less. The banks themselves were not unhappy with this shift to short-term funding, since they saw it as a crude way of cutting their risk without actually reducing credit to the borrower. Mexico alone increased its short-term debt by $2.8 billion in 1979, $8.6 billion in 1980 and $10.9 billion in 1981. By mid-1982 Mexico's short-term debt was equivalent to 15 months' imports, Argentina's to 16 months', Venezuela's to 12 months' and Ecuador's to 11 months'. In total, short-term debt accounted for around $69 billion of Latin America's outstanding external debt of $315 billion at end-1982 – perhaps twice what it should have been under normal conditions.

This high proportion of short-term debt made debt management extremely unstable. By August 1982, Mexico's short-term borrowing had reached crisis proportions. Mexico was nightly borrowing nearly one-quarter of the overnight funds available from the inter-bank market in the United States. The Federal Reserve Board grew concerned at the prospect of an even greater absorption of these funds, and it became clear that drastic action would be needed. Mexico was obliged to agree to a 90-day moratorium on all repayments of principal to the banks, introduce a two-tier exchange rate, and apply to the IMF for a $4 billion loan. On top of this the Falklands war, which culminated with a British victory in June, had already made banks nervous of further lending to the region. The consequence was that from mid-1982 voluntary bank lending to Latin America virtually ceased.

Once the crisis broke, bankers demonstrated a worrying tendency to classify all Latin American countries as equally risky (the same phenomenon which had occurred in 1981 in relation to Eastern Europe after Poland's debt problems finally surfaced). Hence the liquidity problems of Mexico and then Argentina accelerated the cut-back in lending to other borrowers. Take one of the region's smallest borrowers, Uruguay. With a manageable external debt of some $3.3 billion, Uruguay was causing few sleepless nights for international bankers in mid-1982. Yet subsequently it was unable to borrow fresh medium-term money because of the banks' general wariness of Latin America. Believing (quite reasonably) that this situation would be temporary, the Uruguayan authorities accumulated short-term debt. By mid-1983 that, too, was falling due, and with no sign of any revival in competitive lending to Latin America, Uruguay was forced into the very debt-rescheduling which the bankers were so anxious to avoid.

Jonathan Hakim

Structural problems

The shortage of liquid funds with which to service its debt was the immediate cause of Latin America's debt crisis in the summer of 1982. But there was a second, and longer-term, aspect to the problem. A number of structural features of the big Latin American economies contributed to the heavy indebtedness. At the risk of over-simplifying, we shall touch on four of the most important.

First is the pattern of industrialization. The major Latin American countries present a sharp contrast with the other big borrowers in the international capital markets – South-east Asian countries, such as South Korea and the Philippines. The industrialization programmes of these countries have been export-oriented, ensuring that they specialize in goods and services in which they are internationally competitive. This has forced them to generate the maximum amount of foreign exchange per dollar of foreign borrowing. Hence although South Korea's gross external debt stands at about $40 billion – not far short of Argentina's – its debt-service ratio (the proportion of export earnings required to pay interest and principal on the debt) in 1983 was only 24 per cent – against 149 per cent for Argentina. In the larger Latin American countries, export orientation has been a secondary consideration. They have favoured the import-substitution model which, although not necessarily unworkable, was made so by distorted domestic prices caused by government subsidies and high tariff barriers. Many new industries in Latin America have required substantial protection in order to survive. Easy foreign bank loans made it possible to undertake projects whose priorities were primarily political rather than economic – Argentina's paper industry, Venezuela's steel mills, Peru's huge irrigation schemes and Brazil's nuclear power stations (to take just a few examples) were all motivated largely by prestige or employment considerations, neglecting the vital fact that the output which they generated would not be sufficient to repay the capital cost.

Such tendencies have been exacerbated by a second factor – the importance of the state sector. With the exceptions of Chile and Brazil (where public spending declined and remained roughly stable, respectively) public-sector spending increased sharply as a proportion of GDP in Latin America during the 1970s. With revenues failing to match expenditure, public-sector deficits also grew. Brazil's public-sector deficit rose from 2.4 per cent of GDP in 1970 to 6.2 per cent in 1982; Peru's from 0.8 per cent to 8.2 per cent, and Mexico's from 1.9 per cent to 16.9 per cent. Inefficiently (and sometimes corruptly) managed state enterprises were a major reason; in

24

Mexico, for example, the public-enterprise deficit alone stood at around 10 per cent of GDP in 1982. Spending by public enterprises was often subject to little central control, and their revenues were depressed by policies to hold down prices of their output as part of government efforts to combat inflation. The Banco de Mexico recently estimated that if public-sector prices had simply kept pace with inflation the public sector would have actually been in surplus every year between 1965 and 1982, with the exception of 1975.

The consequence of this uncontrolled expansion of the public sector was a crowding-out of private investment (especially in those countries with poorly-developed domestic capital markets). The deficits were financed not just by external debt but also by borrowing from the central bank – which simply increased the rate of monetary growth. In many cases public enterprises had direct access to both sources of finance without even having to seek the permission of the treasury or economy ministry. The result was an explosive build-up of both public-sector debt and of inflation caused by rapid expansion of the money supply.

The third factor is the political prejudice against direct foreign investment. Politicians appear to believe that loans create less 'dependency' than investment, which few Latin American countries have encouraged. Direct investment in Latin America dropped from 30 per cent of capital inflows in the 1960s to 20 per cent by the end of the 1970s. The result is a debt structure which is heavily unbalanced in favour of debt rather than equity. In practice, foreign investors are much more flexible and accommodating than they were 20 years ago. And, as the present debt-servicing problems demonstrate, profit remittances – which require the availability of profits in the first place – may well impose less of a burden than debt-service payments, which do not vary with the profitability of the resulting investment.

Finally there has been a substantial build-up of overseas assets (much of it the result of capital flight) held by residents of the debtor countries. Distorted exchange-rate and interest-rate policies have been an important cause. Overvalued exchange rates in many countries not only worsened their trade deficits but also encouraged local residents to borrow abroad. The distorted exchange rates and artificially low domestic interest rates (often negative in real terms) made foreign-currency-denominated assets seem artificially attractive. And the fact that domestic residents clearly believed such policies were unsustainable provided a further incentive for capital to move abroad. As Table 2.3 demonstrates, the cumulative trade deficits of six big Latin American debtors accounted for less than one-fifth

Table 2.3 *External debt and cumulated changes in balance-of-payments flows, 1974–82 ($ billion)*

	Cumulated increase in gross external debt	Cumulated trade deficit[a]	Cumulated net service and other payments	Cumulated increase in official reserves	Cumulated increase in private claims on non-residents[b]
Argentina	33	−10	20	2	20
Brazil	94	16	68	−1	11
Chile	15	3	10	3	0
Mexico	83	9	37	0	36
Peru	11	1	5	1	3
Venezuela	27	−33	26	9	26
Total	263	14	166	14	96

[a] A minus sign signifies a surplus.
[b] Column 1 less columns 2, 3 and 4.
Source: Federal Reserve Board.

of the gross external debts which they accumulated in 1974–82. Increases in reserves added an insignificant amount. Interest payments were a substantial factor, but the large residual must largely have been accounted for by the accumulation of claims overseas. Moreover since confidence in domestic economic policies was low, little of the income on these overseas assets was repatriated to help service the resulting debts.

Despite the serious policy errors, it would be mistaken to conclude that all of Latin America's external borrowing was frittered away. Gross domestic investment increased significantly as a proportion of GDP during the 1970s for the major Latin American debtor countries, much of it financed by the external borrowing. Nevertheless the present problems would not have been nearly so acute if the policy errors had been avoided.

Debt-management strategies

This, then, is the background to the present crisis. Since August 1982, every Latin American country – with the exception of Colombia and Paraguay – has run into debt-servicing problems. Most are still managing to pay interest – but little more.

Despite the appearance of a multitude of plans for 'solving' the debt crisis, so far the international financial community has stuck firmly to a 'firefighting' approach – seeking individual, *ad hoc* solutions rather than adopting a global strategy.

Most of the schemes for debt reform start with the assumption that the debt problem is not simply a liquidity but a solvency problem. They then go on to argue for a comprehensive restructuring of the debt, usually over very long periods and in most cases involving the creation of one or more government agencies to assume some of the risk on international loans. Part of the reason why such proposals have failed to gather support is the strong political opposition to 'bank bailouts', especially in the United States. More fundamentally, even if the basic premise of a solvency, rather than a liquidity problem is accepted (and this is discussed below) the schemes typically suffer from a number of defects.

a. They do not explicity address the fundamental question of who pays for what is effectively a resource transfer from debtor to creditor countries. Some of the proposals argue that the banks should pay, partly as a penalty for their past over-lending. But this neglects the serious consequences which large-scale debt write-offs would have for bank capital. Others argue that the burden should be assumed by the governments (effectively the taxpayers) of the industrial countries. But again the sums involved are large; although a scheme for simply giving a subsidy to reduce debtor countries' interest payments could conceivably involve manageable sums, taking over and writing off even half the $800 billion owed by LDCs would far outweigh the contributions presently made by the industrial countries to multilateral institutions such as the World Bank and the International Monetary Fund (IMF). Furthermore any resources devoted to debt schemes might well be at the expense of aid budgets for the poorest countries, which have never had access to the international capital markets – an inequitable transfer from poor to middle-income LDCs.

b. Large-scale rescue schemes would tend to remove the incentive for further bank lending to LDCs. One of the main inducements for banks to continue lending (albeit unwillingly) is that fresh loans are necessary to allow the debtors to continue servicing their existing debt. Once that debt was transferred to the balance sheet of some new international agency, this incentive would disappear. In any case, banks would be unlikely to put up new money in the knowledge that it might end up being discounted or put into a long-term bond carrying below-market rates of interest.

c. The establishment of a new agency might encourage LDCs to seek debt relief even if they did not strictly need it – a problem of 'moral hazard'. The more extensive the relief, the greater the incentive for borrowers to deviate from normal commercial relationships with their banks.

Consequently, governments, banks and debtor countries have all so far preferred to stick to *ad hoc* rescheduling-cum-stabilization packages. A standard formula has emerged, comprising six main elements:

1. A short moratorium on principal payments to allow negotiations to take place and prevent individual creditors scrambling to gain an unfair advantage.
2. Bridging loans from the commercial banks and from official sources (usually the Bank for International Settlements, guaranteed by member central banks) to enable immediate obligations to be met.
3. Agreement with the IMF on an economic adjustment programme to reduce the public-sector deficit, adopt more realistic exchange-rate and interest-rate policies and reorient domestic resources towards tradable goods.
4. Agreement with an advisory committee of the main creditor banks and with government creditors through the so-called 'Paris club' to reschedule principal payments falling due in the next one or two years. The standard terms have been to stretch out the payments over six or seven years, including an initial grace period of one or two years during which only interest is payable.
5. New loans from banks and from official creditors (the latter often in the form of export credits).
6. Agreement with creditor banks that a certain minimum level of inter-bank credits be maintained with banks of the debtor country, to ensure that the country can continue to finance its trade.

Before considering the potential problems with this *ad hoc* approach, it is important to be clear about the ultimate aim of any debt-management policy. A proposition which is rather obvious but is all too often overlooked in discussions of external debt is that the debt of a nation is not, as a rule, repaid. This applies just as much to external debt as it does to the internal debt of (for example) the US treasury. Most developing countries, by their very nature, run current-account deficits, which means they are dependent on a continuous inflow of foreign capital. With this inflow, indebtedness rises steadily. The prime objective of debt-management policy, therefore, is not to repay all the outstanding debt – that would require Latin American countries to become consistent net exporters of capital, a political impossibility. Rather the aim must be to reduce the required capital inflows (and hence the growth of external debt) to a level which is economically and financially viable over the medium and longer term.

The question of what constitutes a viable level of external debt for a particular country is unfortunately rather complex. The answer must take

Table 2.4 *External debt service[a] as a percentage of exports of goods and services*

	1975	1976	1977	1978	1979	1980	1981	1982	1983
Latin America									
Service/exports	26.6	29.5	32.4	42.2	43.4	38.3	43.8	59.0[b]	64.6[b]
Interest/exports	13.0	12.9	12.9	16.5	19.2	21.2	26.4	34.3	37.8
Argentina									
Service/exports	31.9	26.3	19.1	41.7	22.9	43.5	53.3	113.0	149.4[b]
Interest/exports	13.3	11.1	7.5	9.5	12.7	21.8	32.0	56.9	56.9
Brazil									
Service/exports	40.8	45.3	48.7	59.3	65.6	63.8	62.8	78.2	82.4[b]
Interest/exports	19.4	19.0	18.7	24.1	31.5	34.1	35.6	45.4	40.7
Chile									
Service/exports	36.2	42.1	47.4	49.0	45.2	43.6	67.2	73.4	62.5[b]
Interest/exports	15.5	13.8	13.8	16.9	16.5	19.3	34.6	48.8	48.8
Colombia									
Service/exports	20.9	18.0	14.1	15.3	20.4	17.7	27.1	35.2	42.9[b]
Interest/exports	10.9	9.2	7.0	7.1	9.5	11.3	10.2	25.5	24.3
Mexico									
Service/exports	38.6	48.8	61.7	66.3	74.8	39.8	44.7	65.4[b]	59.3[b]
Interest/exports	21.1	21.8	22.5	23.3	24.2	23.2	28.8	37.4	42.4
Peru									
Service/exports	31.6	34.1	35.3	40.3	29.5	39.5	58.2	49.8	66.2[b]
Interest/exports	14.6	17.3	14.9	18.8	14.7	16.5	20.5	21.7	31.8
Venezuela									
Service/exports	10.2	10.9	13.5	21.6	25.6	26.4	28.2	32.3	26.6[b]
Interest/exports	4.3	4.5	7.5	13.4	16.0	17.1	18.5	19.4	25.0

[a] Interest and principal payments, excluding amortization of short-term debt.
[b] Portions of these payments have been rescheduled or are outstanding.
Source: Inter-American Development Bank.

into account the entire range of factors determining the country's balance-of-payments position, and therefore cannot be reflected in any one single indicator, such as the widely used debt-service ratio. Although this ratio gives a crude indication of debt burden (see Table 2.4), it does not reflect developments which may be critical to the long-term manageability of the debt. Such developments include the level of import prices, the amount of official development assistance and foreign direct investment inflows and the rate of economic growth in the debtor country. Hence a country-by-country assessment is necessary – and a country-by-country approach to tackling the management of external debt.

Insolvency or illiquidity?

One of the fundamental points of contention in the debate over external debt is whether the problem is one of insolvency or simply one of illiquidity. In company finance this is a fundamental distinction; a private company with debts but still having a positive net worth is said to be illiquid; by contrast a company that simply has negative net worth is said to be insolvent. By analogy, if debtor countries are simply illiquid, then additional lending is the appropriate response to tide them over their difficulties. If, however, they are insolvent, then it may be more appropriate to recognize their debt as simply bad and attempt to salvage at least some portion of it by accepting write-downs – akin to bankruptcy procedures for companies, where creditors simply receive so many cents in the dollar.

The distinction between illiquidity and insolvency is by no means as clear-cut for a country as it is for a private firm, since countries do not go out of business, even if they fail to pay their debts on time. Our analysis of the origins of Latin America's debt problems suggests that the true diagnosis lies somewhere in between, since the blame lies both with unforeseen external economic developments and with poor domestic policies. Furthermore projection models for Latin America assembled by the IMF, the Inter-American Development Bank and others suggest that the debt problem should be controllable over the remainder of the decade by a mixture of more finance from the lenders and economic adjustment by the borrowers – again indicating more of a liquidity than a solvency difficulty.

Such projection models typically make the following assumptions:
1. Although Latin America's imports grow slowly after their precipitous fall in 1982 and 1983, they will be kept well under control by slow economic growth in the debtor countries of under 3 per cent a year in real terms – less than half the rate of the 1970s.
2. Economic growth in the industrial countries averages (somewhat optimistically) 3 per cent a year in real terms for the remainder of the decade.
3. There is no significant increase in protectionism by the industrial countries. This means that every 1 per cent increase in industrial country growth will continue to boost Latin America's exports by 1½ per cent.

4. Dollar interest rates decline gradually in nominal terms from their present levels to around three percentage points lower by 1988–90.
5. There are no further inflationary shocks to the world economy, with real oil prices remaining roughly constant.
6. Net new bank lending to Latin America grows by around 7 per cent a year – roughly the same rate of increase as in 1983.

On these assumptions the models project that Latin America's total external debt will continue increasing in nominal terms (to reach around $430 billion by 1990), but that the debt burden will be progressively reduced. The debt–service ratio would decline from 65:100 in 1983 to under 40:100 by the end of the decade, while the ratio of total external debt to exports would fall from 325:100 to under 200:100.

Potential problems

Those who believe that the *ad hoc* arrangements so far developed for tackling the debt crisis will not prove adequate often argue that the debtor countries cannot be expected to acquiesce in even the relatively favourable scenario outlined above, since it involves a significant net transfer of resources from them to the lenders in the industrial countries. Assuming simply that net new bank lending grows by 7 per cent a year, while interest payments average 12 per cent, they argue that debtor countries would be immediately better off by repudiating their debts – especially if there is little prospect of the banks reverting to voluntary lending (as opposed to the 'forced' lending as part of rescheduling packages).

This incentive to default could be increased by other factors, including:
1. Higher dollar interest rates, lower economic growth in the industrial countries or increased protectionism. Each of these would increase the debt burden, either by raising interest payments or by lowering export revenues.
2. Political reaction in Latin America against IMF-imposed austerity programmes, obliging governments to pursue more expansionary economic policies. This would increase their imports, and consequently their current-account deficits, to unsustainable levels.
3. Refusal of banks to continue increasing their exposure. Banks with relatively small amounts of lending to Latin America might refuse to continue participating in the system of collective lending, on the assumption that their individual action would make no difference to the eventual outcome. This would result in an ever-greater concentration of lending on a small number of big international banks. Already 125 of

Brazil's 830 creditor banks account for 90 per cent of bank lending to that country. A breakdown would lead to increasing instability, as the big banks tied up a growing proportion of their assets in loans to Latin America.

The difficulty with the repudiation argument is that it neglects the element of uncertainty about the consequences of a default. Default (defined as unwillingness to pay for a prolonged period) would not simply involve swapping the loss of new loans for the avoidance of interest payments. The defaulting country would also find itself denied short-term credits by the banks, which would reduce its international trade to a cash or barter basis. Since imports have to be paid for immediately while export receipts are received after a lag, only countries with substantial foreign-exchange reserves could successfully trade on a cash basis – and all Latin American countries' reserves have been heavily depleted by the debt crisis. Furthermore, although the resumption of voluntary lending by banks at present looks a remote prospect for almost all Latin American borrowers, this does not imply that the prospect is ruled out indefinitely. Default would eliminate even the possibility of fresh voluntary loans. A defaulting country could also face legal reprisals; foreign creditors might attach its foreign assets as well as its exports abroad.

All this may explain the surprisingly cooperative stance of Latin American governments so far. A number of big debtor countries have given serious consideration to the possibility of default, and rejected it. The experience of the few countries which have defaulted is not encouraging for them. President Fidel Castro of Cuba, which defaulted in 1961, reportedly told the then Jamaican prime minister Mr Michael Manley in early 1980 that whatever Manley did he should avoid default.

True, a significant number of countries have been in *de facto* default simply by not paying their debts for periods of up to several months – most recently Argentina. But a formal default needs to be declared by the creditors, and so far banks have not exercised their right to do so. This is because the benefits to them of calling a default are likely to be small. The defaulting country's overseas assets which might be seized are likely to be few in relation to its external debt. Furthermore the legal mechanics of default are costly and uncertain, as the lawsuits brought against Costa Rica by Libra Bank (in 1983) and Allied International Bank (in 1984) demonstrated. The attraction of being first in the legal queue for a country's assets does provide an incentive for an individual bank to move first. But so far peer-group pressure from other banks has succeeded in keeping everyone in line.

Nevertheless, if the assumptions of lower interest rates or industrial country growth prove to be over-optimistic – as they may well prove to be – then the banks will have to reconsider the terms on which they are refinancing existing debt. Longer maturities for refinancing may have to be conceded by the banks, and probably also some capitalization of interest payments. (Table 2.5 shows the gross and net debt due to commercial banks, and Table 2.6 illustrates the impact of higher interest rates on Latin America's debt burden.) The latter has been fiercely resisted by the banks, who maintain that charging below-market interest rates would undermine their commercial *raison d'être*. However, if interest rates remain high in real terms (rather than gently declining as widely assumed) then capitalizing interest payments will have to be given serious consideration.

Table 2.5 *Debt due to commercial banks, end-June 1983 ($ billion)*

	Gross	Net of deposits with banks
Argentina	25.5	18.7
Brazil	62.8	57.7
Chile	10.9	8.5
Mexico	65.5	52.1
Peru	5.3	3.0
Venezuela	26.8	13.3

Source: Bank for International Settlements.

Table 2.6 *How a 1 per cent rise in interest rates affects debtor countries*

	Increased payments to banks[a] ($ billion)	Projected 1984 imports ($ billion)	Import cut-back needed to compensate[b] (%)
Argentina	187	4.7	4.0
Brazil	577	16.0	3.6
Chile	85	3.3	2.6
Mexico	521	10.0	5.2
Peru	30	2.7	1.1
Venezuela	133	9.0	1.5

[a] Based on net debt at end-June 1983.
[b] Assuming exports stay unchanged.
Source: Bank for International Settlements, official figures.

Real dollar interest rates are being sustained by:

1. The large public-sector deficit in the United States, accompanied by fears that US inflation will revive if there is any move to monetize the deficit.
2. Tax deductibility of interest payments for many US borrowers, which means that net (after-tax) interest rates for them are very much lower than market rates imply.
3. Deregulation of the American banking system, with an accompanying move to floating-rate loans. Borrowers are prepared to continue borrowing if they believe that interest payments will automatically fall as market rates come down.

None of these factors is likely to disappear in the short term, which strengthens the debtors' argument for some interest-rate relief. Subsidy schemes paid for by the industrial countries are unlikely to be acceptable politically without further increases in interest rates, leading to fears for the safety of American banks. But there are precedents for capitalizing interest payments. Nicaragua persuaded the banks to agree to reschedule interest payments as well as principal in 1980, partly because its economy was shattered by civil war. Banks have also effectively rescheduled interest for Poland by re-lending interest payments in the form of revolving loans for trade credits.

So far the IMF has played a key role in keeping the banks united in support of the various financial rescue packages. But the IMF's resources are limited. Its biggest single loan in Latin America, for example, is the $5.5 billion three-year facility agreed with Brazil in February 1983, and even this provided only one-tenth of Brazil's gross financing requirements in 1983. IMF member countries agreed in 1983 to increase their IMF quotas (on which the Fund's lending capacity is based) by nearly 50 per cent to $97 billion. But this is still a limited amount relative to the size of the LDC debt problem (total outstanding external debt of developing countries at the end of 1983 stood at roughly $800 billion). In consequence, the IMF must rely on its ability to coax the banks into lending more money to a country by bestowing its so-called 'seal of approval' on the country's economic pro-gramme. This tactic seems to be working.

The IMF has in many cases withheld its agreement to an economic adjustment programme until virtually all the country's creditor banks have committed themselves to participating in a fresh loan. This pressure has been reinforced by pressure from central banks and from the large banks who conduct the negotiations with the debtor country, and who have most to lose from the breakdown of the rescue strategy. By such methods, virtually all of Brazil's 830 creditor banks were induced to participate in a new loan of $6.5 billion designed to provide Brazil's new-money requirements for 1984. However, many senior bankers doubt whether this technique can be repeated indefinitely. More incentive might have to be provided to smaller banks to participate – perhaps including inferior repayment terms for those banks which stay out of future loans.

A debtors' cartel?

Despite the reluctance so far of the debtor countries to repudiate their debt, some of the more radical rhetoric in Latin America has suggested that the countries should unite to demand more favourable repayment terms from the banks, using the threat of default as a bargaining counter.

The consequences of an outright repudiation by all the big Latin American borrowers would certainly be crippling for the banks – and for American banks in particular. The American banks have loans of over $80 billion to Latin America, with the nine largest American money-centre banks alone accounting for $50 billion. In 1983, the combined gross (before tax) profits of these nine banks was around $5.2 billion. Setting aside 10 per cent of their loans to Latin America as provisions each year would therefore wipe out virtually the whole of their annual profits. Furthermore a number of big American banks derive a significant proportion of their total profits from local subsidiaries in Latin America, quite apart from their cross-border loans to the countries. For example in 1983 Citicorp, the world's biggest bank, obtained one-fifth of its global profits from its operation in Brazil. The magnitude of these figures is such that, in practice, a large-scale debt repudiation would almost inevitably bring about some form of intervention by the central banks of the industrial countries to avert a widespread banking crisis.

In view of the consequences, and of the fact that creditors would have greater difficulties in taking reprisals against a coalition of debtor countries than against a single unilateral defaulter, the idea of a debtors' cartel has some superficial appeal. But the debtors have widely differing interests. The appeal of the cartel is greatest to the smaller borrowers, who individually have the least leverage in their negotiations with the banks. The larger debtors have remained anxious to preserve their credit rating as best they can in the hope that they will at some stage again be able to attract net capital inflows from the banks. So even if one country took the lead by repudiating its debt it is not clear that others would follow. The debtor countries do increasingly consult each other on rescheduling terms and conditions on an informal basis. But the formation of a full-blooded debtors' cartel looks unlikely.

Conclusions

The present financial crisis in Latin America can be traced back to the aftermath of the second oil shock in 1979 and is rooted in both external and internal problems. Consequently a delicate combination of domestic economic adjustment, fresh finance, and external economic growth will be necessary if the crisis is to be overcome.

So far the easiest part of the adjustment process has been completed – a turn-round in Latin America's balance of payments achieved almost entirely through a severe contraction in imports. In 1983 Latin America's imports dropped by 21 per cent following a 22 per cent contraction the previous year. For some individual countries (such as Mexico) the decline has been even steeper. The most difficult part of the adjustment process – restoring economic growth through increased exports – is still to come.

Despite some encouraging signs (such as a 22 per cent rise in Brazil's exports in the first half of 1984) it remains questionable how far this can be achieved. The critical factor will be the rate of economic growth in the industrial countries. Although the United States' economy displayed a strong performance in 1983, growing at over 3 per cent, with a 5 per cent real growth rate predicted for 1984, so far the European economies have been slow to respond. There are justifiable fears that the recovery will prove to be only weak. Such an outcome would clearly jeopardize Latin America's export prospects and hence its ability to service its debts without further, politically unacceptable, austerity measures. In order to avoid this outcome, economic policy in the industrial countries will have to be shifted away from the simple focus on inflation-fighting towards promoting steady and non-inflationary growth. And fiscal deficits in the developed countries (especially the United States) will have to be reduced in order to lower interest rates. This will not be easy.

For the present, default (i.e. repudiation) on external debt is not in the interests of either borrowers or lenders. However, many Latin American sovereign borrowers have at times been in undeclared default through non-payment of interest or principal on their loans – a situation sometimes of many months' duration. If the adjustment process breaks down (and it will easily do so if the outlook continues to be for low growth, protectionism and high real interest rates) then we are more likely to witness a process of 'default by attrition' rather than outright debt repudiation. This would take the form of repeated failure by debtor countries to meet the terms of their IMF programmes and rescheduling agreements, resulting in a virtually endless series of renegotiations, with banks, borrowers and the IMF jockeying for position in a costly and time-consuming ritual. The most damaging aspects of such a breakdown would be a declining credibility of the IMF and an increasing reluctance on the part of banks to provide fresh loans to the borrowers. This in turn would make the downward spiral even more difficult to halt.

The only favourable element in such a scenario would be that it might give banks a breathing-space in which to write down their loan portfolios to more realistic levels. But the accompanying uncertainty might also provoke funding crises for them such as the one which brought down Continental Illinois over its domestic lending in May 1984.

Even on the best possible outlook the Latin American debt problem will not disappear overnight. An encouraging development has been the realization by the industrial countries that continued difficulty for the debtors is against their own self-interest, since it hurts their export markets and is a destabilizing influence on the financial system. Protracted austerity in the developing world provides a deflationary bias to the world economy which all sides have a vested interest in removing.

Despite the continued uncertainty over its eventual outcome, some lessons of the debt crisis are already apparent. Banks have become more prudent in their lending, placing more emphasis on financing specific projects rather than on amorphous balance-of-payments loans. Borrowers have been made painfully aware of the ultimate price of poor domestic policies. They are belatedly making efforts both to increase domestic savings (to compensate for reduced availability of bank lending from abroad) and to redress the balance between debt and equity in their borrowings. Governments in the industrial countries (and particularly in the United States) have realized the value of strong multilateral organizations, such as the World Bank and IMF. And all the actors in the international lending game – banks, borrowers, central banks, and multilateral organizations – have learned to cooperate in an unprecedented manner.

The business of financing development is at last seen to be more complex and long-term than many of the parties (especially the banks) have so far acknowledged. Let us hope they have learned some valuable lessons about what kind of development is appropriate, and how it should be financed in the future.

3 A Comparison of Macroeconomic Strategies in South America*

JOHN WILLIAMSON†

There are few areas of the world in which macroeconomic policy has been as innovative as in South America over the past quarter-century. The rest of the world, the developed and even more the developing, has much to learn from study of this rich variety of experience.

In the 1950s most South American countries pursued expansionary fiscal and monetary policies and import-substituting industrialization, as advocated by the Economic Commission for Latin America (ECLA). The inflationary strains that resulted were validated by passive monetary policies and rationalized as the result of structural imbalances. This strategy was rather successful during the 1950s, but by the early 1960s it was reaching its two natural limits. First, although import-substituting industrialization is initially a sensible policy for developing countries because the first industries established tend to be labour-intensive, further stages of industrialization involve moving on from non-durable consumer goods into consumer durables and capital goods, and these industries require skilled labour, exhibit greater economies of scale, and are more capital-intensive, so that they are less suited to countries at an early stage of industrialization. Secondly, the maintenance of a high level of internal demand led not only to payments deficits but also to accelerating inflation. These problems prompted the periodic adoption of 'orthodox' stabilization programmes involving monetary and fiscal restraint and devaluation, in order to restore the balance of payments and a measure of price stability. However, successive stabilization programmes became progressively less effective in restoring price stability as expectations and institutions adjusted to chronic variable inflation.

Economic policies began to diverge around the middle of the 1960s. The following sections of this chapter sketch and compare the evolution of policies in four major countries: Colombia, Brazil, Chile, and Argentina.

* This chapter, based on the presentation given to the Latin America study group at Chatham House, appeared in ODI's *Development Policy Review*, 1, no. 1 (May 1983).
† The author is indebted to William R. Cline for valuable comments.

Colombia

Colombia pioneered the transition from emphasis on import substitution to export promotion around 1967. The futile attempt to maintain a fixed exchange rate while inflation ran faster than that abroad was abandoned in favour of a crawling peg, which crawled with a view to roughly neutralizing the external effects of the excess domestic inflation. This resulted in maintaining much greater (although not absolute) constancy of the real exchange rate. Tariffs were not reduced to a point which threatened the viability of existing industries, but the previous policy of giving whatever protection was needed in order to establish new industries was abandoned, and instead export incentives were provided to the existing industries.

Colombian macroeconomic policy during the 1970s can be characterized as broadly Keynesian, at least if one associates Keynes with the attempt to stabilize rather than with a determination to expand irrespective of circumstances. In the 1977 boom (based on the high coffee prices caused by the Brazilian frosts, which reinforced the booming trade in narcotics) the government ran a large budget surplus, and in consequence the economy maintained a large surplus on current account. Reserves were built up to very high levels, so that even today Colombian reserves are two-thirds of its external debt. While the real exchange rate was allowed to appreciate to some extent in order to limit the inflationary impact of the payments surplus, the major emphasis of policy was on preserving a sufficiently competitive exchange rate to avoid the destruction of the newly created industrial export sector. Periods of lower inflationary pressure were exploited to improve the competitiveness of domestic industry by devaluing somewhat faster than the inflation differential. For a decade Colombia enjoyed high rates of growth with inflation which, while persistently high (fluctuating around a figure of about 30 per cent), never got out of hand.

At the present time, growth in Colombia, as in most of the world, has ground to a standstill. This is mainly the result of weak demand in external markets, as reflected particularly in the low price of coffee and in consequence of import-substitution by the consumers of narcotics, reinforced by intermittent attempts to combat a deeply embedded inflation. Even good economic management cannot avoid the constraints imposed by external events.

Brazil

The Brazilian 'economic miracle' of 1967–73 involved real growth rates of some 10 per cent per annum combined with a strong external-payments position and a rate of inflation that fell to some 20 per cent per annum, which was modest by Brazilian if not by international standards. The main elements supporting this performance were the substantial excess capacity created by the preceding stabilization programme, which provided considerable scope for cyclical recovery; forcible repression of wage levels; aggressive investment by state enterprises; and the adoption of outward-looking policies (a crawling peg which depreciated fast enough to maintain competitiveness, combined with export subsidies for non-traditional – mainly manufactured – exports, and some liberalization of import protection). The Second National Development Plan adopted in 1974 blithely assumed that such rates of growth could continue through the 1970s, but events soon proved that this was over-optimistic. The second oil shock combined with the exhaustion of cyclical slack and the decision to move toward political liberalization (which required modification of the previous policy of wage repression) to make the boom unsustainable in 1974. The consequences were a renewed acceleration of inflation and a very heavy deficit on the current account of the balance of payments.

For the next five years Brazilian macroeconomic policy rather resembled the British stop-go policies of the 1960s – with the important difference that the trend rate of growth was 7 per cent per annum rather than 3 per cent. The current-account deficit was large throughout the period, but it was financed without difficulty by borrowing from foreign banks. A new long-term programme of import-substitution was adopted, with the idea that growth would be sustained by foreign borrowing until the long-term programme reached fruition.

The change of president in 1979 brought a struggle for economic power between Mario Simonsen, who had concluded that there was no longer any chance of avoiding a real stabilization programme, and Delfim Netto, the architect of the earlier miracle and apostle of growth at any price. Delfim won in the summer of 1979 and promptly initiated a 'dash for growth'. Unfortunately for Brazil, this policy switch occurred at a time when the economy was not only fully employed but also subjected to the second oil shock, a poor harvest, and a victory for the campaign of the Minister of Labour to introduce biannual in place of annual wage indexation (with, moreover, a formula which gave more than full compensation for inflation to low-income wage earners). At the end of 1979 the government decreed a maxi-devaluation of the cruzeiro with the object of improving the balance of payments. However, any possible impact in that direction was quickly nullified by a venture into the then fashionable attempt to fight inflation by changing expectations, which was supposed to be accomplished by the announcement that depreciation would be limited to a maximum of 40 per cent in the course of 1980. In fact inflation exploded to a peak rate of well over 100 per cent per annum in 1980–1, while Brazil's previously excellent credit-worthiness eroded rapidly.

In the course of 1980 it became apparent that these heterodox policies were failing. Policy was vigorously thrown into reverse, with renewed efforts to limit government spending and monetary expansion, and elimination of the ceiling on depreciation. The policy reversal only just avoided the necessity for Brazil to resort to the IMF at the end of 1980, an act which in Brazil is considered to be the ultimate political disgrace.

But it also produced an unprecedented recession (in Brazilian terms) in 1981, with a fall in GNP now estimated at between 2 and 4 per cent (in comparison with the trend growth of some 7 per cent). The balance of trade duly moved back into modest surplus as a result of the fall in imports and the vigorous expansion in exports. The benefit of this for the current account was, however, largely neutralized by the world rise in interest rates. Brazil's current-account deficit is seriously overstated by conventional accounting practices, which make no allowance for the fact that a part of interest payments merely compensate for inflation, and thus should really be counted as amortization under inflation accounting. But even after adjusting for this factor, the current-account deficit remained at something like 3 per cent of GNP.

In 1982 the balance of payments underwent contrary influences, with a recession-induced decline in imports going some way to compensate for the fall in the value of exports caused by very weak export prices of primary commodities and the cut-back in demand in Brazil's major markets for manufactured exports in the developing countries. While output has stopped falling, there has not as yet been any significant recovery. Borrowing was on a hand-to-mouth basis even before the Mexican crisis, after which it completely dried up, at least temporarily. At worst, Brazil may face a major financial crisis before this is read; at best, it is difficult to see that the government will have significant scope for stimulating the economy until world demand revives.

Chile

Although Chile was the first country to adopt a crawling peg, in 1965, it maintained the policy of import-substituting industrialization through the 1960s, in line with the structuralist theoretical framework of the dominant technocrats. From 1970 to 1973 there was the brief attempt at a democratic transition to socialism under Allende, an attempt which was not aided by technical stupidities such as allowing the exchange rate to become unrealistic or the introduction of an impossibly complex multiple-rate system with differences of as much as a hundred times between one rate and another.

The counter-revolutionary Pinochet government was staffed by Chicago-trained monetarists. When they first came to office their dominant ideology was that of old-style Friedmanian monetarism, which looked to control of the money supply to regulate inflation and sought a realistic exchange rate in order to achieve payments equilibrium. However, after about 1978 the dominant orthodoxy became the global monetarism of Johnson and Mundell, in which a fixed (or at least predetermined path for the) exchange rate is regarded as the critical mechanism for determining inflation, while credit control is manipulated to support the maintenance of the planned exchange rate and the money supply is allowed to adjust passively. Fiscal policy has to be sufficiently disciplined to avoid undermining the desired credit control. Beyond that, the task of government is to free markets and allow prices to determine resource allocation, a policy which was vigorously followed in Chile with measures that included large-scale denationalization, drastic reduction of trade barriers, and liberalization of capital inflows.

For several years in the late 1970s Chile achieved high rates of growth of some 8 per cent per annum, together with a strong balance-of-payments position and declining inflation. Along with Argentina and Britain, the Chilean experience was held up as an example of successful monetarism in action. But by 1981 problems were becoming evident. The current account went into large deficit, which was indeed financed by a capital inflow – but only because of astronomic real interest rates inside Chile, which led to a severe domestic recession, especially in the construction sector. Inflation did indeed converge to the international level as the theory had said it should, but only after a large overvaluation of the Chilean peso had emerged. The capital inflow was largely used to bid up the prices of domestic real assets, which depressed domestic savings since the wealth-owning classes regarded the appreciation in the value of their assets as a substitute for new savings.

There was considerable discussion in early 1982 as to whether a devaluation was not needed. The arguments in favour were that the peso had become substantially overvalued and that the attempt to sustain a fixed rate in the face of widespread scepticism was responsible for the high interest rates. Monetarists replied that devaluation would be quickly neutralized by inflationary wage increases, especially given the indexation arrangements, while the high real interest rates reflected a shortage of real capital and not a risk premium needed to compensate for the probability of devaluation. In early 1982 the government maintained the exchange rate fixed and inflation was actually negative, though not by enough to make a serious dent in the overvaluation.

The government relented from its tough stand in June 1982, when the peso was devalued by 15 per cent. The wage-indexation formula was modified to minimize the danger of the devaluation being neutralized by inflation, but even so a significant positive rate of inflation again emerged. The initial devaluation did not serve to reduce interest rates: on the contrary, a run on the peso developed, since the devaluation undermined the credibility of the commitment to maintain a fixed rate. The authorities soon concluded that the situation was not viable and they allowed the peso to float – whereupon it depreciated sharply – and reimposed exchange controls. At that point real interest rates fell back to normal levels, thus indicating that the earlier high real rates were indeed in large measure an exchange-risk premium. Competitiveness has thus been regained, which should position the economy to take advantage of any international upturn that may materialize. But at the moment the economy remains in a deep recession while inflation is back in double digits. Monetarism did not provide a quick-fix solution to the problems that have plagued economic managers of more orthodox persuasion.

Argentina

Argentine economic policy has lurched more violently and frequently from one extreme to another than that of Brazil or Chile – or, perhaps, of any other country in the world. One of the few constants prior to the mid-1970s was the continued pursuit of policies of import-substitution, which was carried to the point where virtually the whole range of consumer goods become *de facto* non-tradables. In other respects policy varied from the most rigid of orthodox stabilization programmes to the expansionist populism of the Peróns (1945–53, 1973–6). Isabel Perón was displaced by a military coup in 1976 as inflation reached an annual rate of some 700 per cent.

The military junta followed the example of their Chilean neighbours in appointing Chicago-trained or at least Chicago-oriented economists to critical positions. As in Chile, the resulting policies reflected the teachings of the Chicago School and especially, as of December 1978, the doctrines of international monetarism. There was a drastic reduction of tariffs, liberalization of the capital account (including convertibility of the peso), and the

43

announcement of a table showing the value of the dollar exchange rate over a future period of several months. The rate of devaluation was set below the domestic rate of inflation and reduced over time, with the aim of reaching a fixed rate at the end of the government's term of office in early 1981. The basic idea was again to use the discipline of the Law of One Price* in order to reduce inflation.

There turned out to be two fatal flaws in the strategy adopted. The first was that the Argentine military, unlike their Chilean counterparts, did not have the determination necessary to reduce the fiscal deficit to a level that would have been consistent with the rate of credit expansion implied by the tapering rate of devaluation: Argentina continued to need the inflation tax. The second was that the Argentine price system, just like the Chilean, did not obey the Law of One Price. Inflationary inertia was overcome by the forces of arbitrage only slowly, as a large overvaluation of the peso emerged, rather than more or less immediately, as the theory had predicted.

In the mean time there emerged a large gap between the real rate of interest as perceived by Argentine borrowers (negative) and the real return as perceived by foreign lenders (strongly positive). As long as that gap persisted and as long as the belief in the credibility of the exchange-rate commitment was maintained, foreign lenders had an incentive to make loans to Argentina and Argentinians found it attractive to borrow, so that there was a vast capital inflow, which expanded the money supply and so tended to increase inflation rather than diminish it. By 1980 the Argentinian peso had become seriously overvalued but this was not perceived by the government. Most firms did not believe the situation to be sustainable and therefore assumed that relief would come fairly quickly if only they could avoid bankruptcy, and because of the expense of dismissing workers there was little increase in unemployment during this period. Indeed, the incentive to borrow at almost any cost was so strong that it is said that business firms which owned banks raised the interest rate paid to depositors in order to attract funds which could then be used in order to keep their enterprises afloat, a practice which did not frighten off depositors since there was universal and complete insurance of bank deposits by the Central Bank. When inflation fell, as it eventually did once the overvaluation had become sufficiently large, this mechanism led to impossibly high real interest rates, which threatened the financial viability of virtually every productive enterprise in the country.

* 'Global monetarists' assume that *all* prices are determined in the international market because virtually all goods are internationally tradable. Therefore devaluation of national currency is a self-defeating exercise, since this will merely push up the domestic price and cause more inflation. In other words, each good has only 'one price'. (Ed.)

The situation that was built up as a result of these policies was even more clearly unsustainable than that in Chile, primarily because the fiscal deficit was never brought under control. Hence there was much nervousness as the time for a change of government approached in early 1981. The outgoing administration attempted to pre-empt speculation by announcing a small (10 per cent) devaluation, but the effect was rather to undermine the credibility of the promise to maintain the announced schedule of devaluation, and so a run on the peso developed. The new government responded with a succession of massive devaluations, experiments with a dual exchange market, and recently the renunciation of free-market principles: price and interest-rate controls have returned, and exchange control has been restored. The series of measures adopted have not prevented the collapse of confidence, widespread bankruptcies, falling output and rising unemployment, and a reacceleration of inflation to some 170 per cent per annum. But it should also be said that the real exchange rate has fallen to a very competitive level and a large trade surplus has once more emerged (aided by the fall in imports as a result of declining output) – facts which underline the débâcle of the monetarist experiment, inasmuch as the underlying theory had denied that the real exchange rate depends on changes in the nominal rate.

Following the loss of the Falklands War and the Mexican crisis, Argentina is now seeking a debt-rescheduling and negotiating with the IMF for a standby. Economic chaos has reached a point unique even in the history of that troubled country.

Lessons to be learned

In drawing lessons from recent events in South America, it is important to avoid the temptation to attribute guilt by association. Despite the current difficulties of the region, there is little analytical reason to judge the turn towards outwardly oriented trade policies over the last 15 years a failure, or to justify a call for reversion to the old strategy of import-substitution. Capital-market liberalization has been less of a success than trade liberalization: complete liberalization as in Argentina has exposed macroeconomic policy to strong external influences, which have often proved disruptive as a consequence of both the interaction with exchange-rate policy and apparent market myopia. Even the partial liberalization involved in borrowing from the international capital market while maintaining exchange controls (as in Brazil) looks of questionable wisdom with hindsight from October 1982, although *ex ante*, when one assumed that a certain continuity in

Northern policy-making could be taken for granted, it seemed reasonable enough.

But without question the most striking lessons that can be learned relate to the failure of monetarist strategies of economic management. By a monetarist macroeconomic strategy I understand one which attempts to limit the government's role in the economy to the restricting of some critical monetary variable to a non-inflationary growth path, and beyond that relies on free markets to guide the allocation of resources and the evolution of the macroeconomy. In the Southern Cone monetarist experiments of Argentina and Chile (and Uruguay) the monetary variable whose path was controlled was the exchange rate. In the Northern Hemisphere the chosen variable has of course been some measure of the money supply rather than the exchange rate. But this difference is less important than the similarities, specifically the assumption that the Law of One Price can be relied upon to provide an effective brake upon inflation through the external sector so that large distortions in relative prices do not arise. What the experience of the Southern Cone has demonstrated above all else is that the assumption is too facile to be relied upon for policy purposes, which should not surprise those who knew that previous research had demonstrated beyond all doubt that the Law of One Price is not descriptively accurate.[1] Inflationary inertia has led to massive overvaluation wherever the monetarist counter-inflationary strategy has been adopted. The resulting distortions in relative prices led to intolerable strains on the balance of payments, first in Argentina, and subsequently in Chile. Once the predetermined path of the exchange rate was abandoned, confidence evaporated and a crisis of epic proportions was unleashed, especially in Argentina.

This cannot be brushed aside as an accident due to unexpected exogenous shocks, although it is true that the rise in the dollar (to which the Chilean peso was pegged) and the fall in the copper price did accentuate the difficulties in Chile. But the peso had become overvalued even before those shocks – as it had to, since the strategy relies on downward arbitrage pressure from the prices of foreign goods in order to curtail inflation. The problem is that liberalization to allow the market to work its magic does not secure something close to a unique set of equilibrium relative prices. Theorists have in fact known for a long time that confidence in the uniqueness of equilibrium relative prices is ill-founded. What the experiences of the Southern Cone have demonstrated more graphically than ever before is that there is in reality a great deal of elasticity in the relative price structure. Changes in nominal variables, notably the exchange rate, have a profound impact on real variables, like the real exchange rate; and a lack of change in the nominal exchange rate in the presence of inflationary inertia can lead to grossly distorted relative prices, with catastrophic consequences.

This is a lesson whose implications stretch far beyond South America. For too long the debate on markets, prices and macroeconomic management has been polarized between those who believe that prices do not matter because they have little impact on behaviour and those who believe that all that is necessary to secure a correct price structure is to liberalize markets. But there is a third possible position, which is that prices are profoundly important but that markets cannot in general be trusted to set them. This is a position which implies that a major aim of macroeconomic policy should be to manipulate policy instruments with the object of achieving appropriate values for variables like the real exchange rate, the real wage, the real interest rate, and the profit rate. It is a position which has received powerful support from events in the Southern Cone.

Colombian experience demonstrates that consistent counter-cyclical management and a concern to maintain appropriate relative prices can play a worthwhile stabilizing role. (The contrast with Brazil demonstrates the importance of consistency.) Such management cannot insulate a country from the major trends in the world economy, but the Colombian example does suggest that Keynesian macroeconomic management, even when combined with sub-optimal trade and distributional policies, can avoid the absolute declines in output and financial crises that have recently afflicted all three of their Southern Cone neighbours.

NOTE

1 See in particular the evidence of the Symposium on Purchasing Power Parity published in the *Journal of International Economics*, May 1978.

4 Latin American and East Asian NICs: Development Strategies Compared

GUSTAV RANIS and LOUISE ORROCK

The newly industrializing countries (NICs) of Latin America have, until recently, achieved surprisingly high rates of economic growth. Even after the first oil shock in 1973, the Latin American NICs were able to maintain respectable growth rates by increasing their foreign borrowing, and their active demand for Western goods helped to soften the impact of world recession. They were less successful after 1979, however, in adjusting to the second round of inflation, which was accompanied by high real interest rates and increasing protectionism. The problems of the Latin American countries have become more acute in the past two to three years; because OPEC surpluses have virtually disappeared, while at the same time debtor countries have found it increasingly difficult to repay even the interest on previous debt, commercial banks are now both less able and less willing to make fresh loans available. Growth among the Latin American countries has ground to a halt, and their massive external debts appear to threaten the stability of the international financial system.

Yet it would be wrong to attribute these difficulties entirely to the state of the world economy or to seek their solution by calling either for tougher IMF stabilization programmes or for increased international liquidity. The unfavourable world economic environment has merely highlighted problems inherent in the basic economic development path of these countries but previously masked by the extraordinary global prosperity of the early post-war era.

It is worth distinguishing between the Latin American and East Asian NICs. Although growth rates were similar in both groups until recently, substantial differences are now emerging which had previously been masked by rising world growth rates and, after 1973, by the ability of the Latin American countries to attract large foreign loans. The East Asian NICs have faced the same problems in the world economy but have coped reasonably well since 1979, with only slightly reduced growth rates and without serious debt problems. Moreover, throughout the entire post-war period, the East Asian NICs have been far more successful in reducing poverty and unemployment.

This chapter will examine the East Asian development pattern in an attempt to discover why these countries have apparently been able to achieve growth with equity as well as, more recently, adapting to continued global recession, protectionism and high interest rates. It will then review the typical development pattern of the Latin American NICs and present reasons for their generally relatively poorer performance. Finally, it will suggest some possible policy considerations.

II

Any attempt to compare groups of countries risks concealing as much as it reveals: important and instructive differences occur within any group, including the East Asian NICs. Nevertheless, a study of the past thirty years of development in the four East Asian countries, Hong Kong, Singapore, South Korea and Taiwan, does reveal strong underlying similarities, both in their original condition and in their subsequent mode of generating economic growth, all of which suggests that it is valid to generalize about the East Asian experience and to compare it with that of other developing countries.[1] This section will focus mainly on Taiwan and South Korea, because Hong Kong and Singapore, while members of the same group in most respects, are really city states whose size and relative absence of any agricultural sector make them extremely special, and their development pattern therefore less relevant to other developing countries.

All four countries are densely populated and poor in natural resources. They also share a cultural tradition which by the early 1950s had resulted in a high level of literacy and basic education among the large surplus labour force. Moreover, all four are relatively small, so that, given an abundance of high-quality labour and scarce natural resources, the international aspects of development – especially trade and capital flows – were likely to feature prominently.

By the early 1950s, both South Korea and Taiwan had a reasonably well-developed agricultural sector. While Taiwan possessed a rather more favourable climate, soil and potential for multiple cropping and technological innovation, both countries had benefited from the Japanese colonial investments in the rural sector, including the improvement of irrigation and the creation of farmers' organizations, in order to increase the production of food crops required by the mother country. There was also a fairly equal

49

distribution of assets, especially land, in both countries – thanks to earlier Japanese reforms and subsequent, post-war, legislation. The distribution of land in Taiwan, for example, was roughly twice as equitable as in the rest of the developing world, including Latin America.

In Taiwan, during the colonial period, the agricultural sector produced the domestic food supply as well as traditional land-based exports (mainly rice and sugar) which helped to finance the import of manufactured non-durables, such as textiles. Korea differed slightly, in that it relied to a greater extent on mineral exports.

In the early 1950s, the East Asian NICs entered the customary first stage of post-colonial economic development by adopting a strategy of import-substituting industrialization. This began in Taiwan in about 1951 and South Korea in about 1952. Both countries continued to export traditional products (mainly cash crops in the case of Taiwan, while in South Korea, too, agricultural exports became increasingly important relative to mineral exports). But a part of the revenue from these exports was diverted from the purchase of non-durable manufactured imports to the purchase of producer goods (capital goods and processed raw materials) destined for emerging domestic industries whose production of non-durable consumer goods for the home market gradually replaced previous imports.

During this import-substitution phase, foreign trade declined as a proportion of national income because the policies associated with import-substitution favoured the domestic market and the protection of these new industries. Because of their long-run scarcity of natural resources, large surpluses of unskilled labour and good levels of education, the mobilization of human resources in the industrial process became increasingly important in the East Asian countries. Traditional populations were converted into modern factory workers; agricultural and commercial entrepreneurs were gradually turned into industrial entrepreneurs and managers, capable of applying modern science and technology; and civil servants, previously occupied in maintaining law and order, focused their attention on the promotion of economic development. Once the necessary skills had been acquired, East Asian industries would be able to compete successfully in international markets. In the mean time, however, policies were directed towards supporting industrial production for the domestic market, often with the help of foreign capital.

During the import-substitution phase, government policy is usually strongly protectionist. Because domestic industry is guaranteed profits even in the absence of productive efficiency, and because of distorted price signals, the industrial process, in terms of the choice of goods produced, often remains inefficient – that is, prematurely skilled-labour-, capital- and technology-intensive. In addition, there tends to result a neglect of the rural sector, and, in particular, of food-producing agriculture. What is note-worthy in the case of the East Asian countries is that they adopted a relatively mild version of import-substitution. They paid more attention to the rural economy[2] and protected new industries less than was typical. Although the usual protectionist devices were adopted, including tariffs, import-licensing, overvalued exchange rates, and artificially low interest rates, their implementation in the East Asian countries was less severe, more flexible and more short-lived than in other developing countries.

Growth rates were high in South Korea and Taiwan during the first years of import-substitution but began to fall in both countries during the second half of the 1950s. The initial phase of import-substitution will eventually fail to sustain the same rate of economic growth; once the home market for non-durable goods is being supplied entirely by domestic industry, any further industrialization must slow to the pace of population and per-capita income change.

At this point, a choice has to be made between, on the one hand, maintaining import-substitution but shifting to the production of pre-viously imported producer goods and durable consumer goods, or, on the other hand, commencing to export the same non-durable consumer goods previously supplied mainly to the home market. The East Asian countries, after a good deal of hesitation, chose the latter; the initial import-substi-tution phase came to an end in Taiwan about 1961 and in South Korea about 1964.

During this new 'export-substitution' phase, the basis of comparative advantage in trade moves from land to unskilled labour; exports of manu-factured goods become increasingly important relative to agricultural and mineral exports. In both Taiwan and South Korea, industrial exports accounted for roughly 75 per cent of total exports by the end of the 1960s (Tables 4.1a, b, c). Moreover, the decline in trade as a proportion of national income was reversed – exports' share of GDP was soon sub-stantially higher (Table 4.2). Export-substitution led to a greater integra-tion of the East Asian economies into the world economy, in terms not only of the spectacular expansion of trade but also of increasing inflows of private capital, despite the considerable political and strategic uncertainties in the region.

The rate of labour reallocation from agriculture to industry also increased markedly in Taiwan and South Korea during this period because of the high rate of growth of labour-intensive industrial production now destined for

Table 4.1a *Agricultural exports' share in total exports, E_a/E (per cent)*

East Asian NICs	1950	1955	1960	1965	1970	1975	1977
Taiwan	87.9[a]	84.9	51.7	57.9	22.5	17.5	13.4
South Korea	23.1	34.7	51.4	25.3	16.7	15.1	9.7[b]
Hong Kong	30.4[c]	22.9	14.3	10.9	2.6	2.2	2.6[b]
Singapore	—	57.8[d]	61.6	44.5	44.7	22.0	21.9[b]

Latin American NICs	1950	1955	1960	1965	1970	1975	1977
Mexico	53.5	56.6	64.1	64.7	48.8	38.1	39.0
Colombia	83.1[a]	87.6	78.9	75.3	81.2	71.7	76.9
Chile	10.5	6.7	2.8	7.6[c]	7.5	17.3	22.0
Brazil	96.5[f]	95.4	88.9	80.8	75.2	57.9	50.0[b]

[a] Based on figures for 1951. [d] Based on figures for 1956.
[b] Based on figures for 1979. [e] Based on figures for 1966.
[c] Based on figures for 1952. [f] Based on figures for 1953.
Source: UN, *Yearbook of International Trade Statistics.*

Table 4.1b *Mineral exports' share in total exports E_m/E (per cent)*

East Asian NICs	1950	1955	1960	1965	1970	1975	1977
Taiwan	3.8[a]	0.6	2.1	0.4	0.7	1.1	1.6
South Korea	70.9	49.7	8.3	22.7	8.3	7.9	8.1[b]
Hong Kong	2.8[c]	3.8	7.4	2.9	1.9	0.8	0.8[b]
Singapore	—	19.3[d]	12.7	17.4	25.6	36.3	27.4[b]

Latin American NICs	1950	1955	1960	1965	1970	1975	1977
Mexico	38.6	36.3	24.0	22.3	21.2	32.4	34.6
Colombia	16.3[a]	11.4	18.9	18.0	10.8	7.7	4.1
Chile	80.7	87.8	89.5	88.1[c]	88.3	77.1	67.9
Brazil	2.7[f]	2.9	8.1	11.7	14.3	16.7	16.5[b]

[a] Based on figures for 1951. [d] Based on figures for 1956.
[b] Based on figures for 1979. [e] Based on figures for 1966.
[c] Based on figures for 1952. [f] Based on figures for 1953.
Source: UN, *Yearbook of International Trade Statistics.*

Table 4.1c *Manufactured exports' share in total exports, E_i/E (per cent)*

East Asian NICs	1950	1955	1960	1965	1970	1975	1978
Taiwan	8.3[a]	14.5	46.2	41.7	76.8	81.4	84.9
South Korea	6.4	16.0	40.3	52.0	74.9	76.8	81.9[b]
Hong Kong	66.8[c]	73.3	77.9	85.7	95.3	96.7	96.5[b]
Singapore	—	16.8[d]	19.7	28.9	26.7	39.9	43.7[b]
Latin American NICs	1950	1955	1960	1965	1970	1975	1978
Mexico	7.7	7.0	11.9	13.0	30.0	29.5	26.2
Colombia	0.5[a]	0.8	1.4	6.7	8.0	20.6	18.6[e]
Chile	1.1	0.1	3.1	4.2[f]	4.0	5.3	9.7[e]
Brazil	0.7[g]	1.2	2.9	7.5	9.7	23.3	32.6[b]

[a] Based on figures for 1951.   [e] Based on figures for 1977.
[b] Based on figures for 1979.   [f] Based on figures for 1966.
[c] Based on figures for 1952.   [g] Based on figures for 1953.
[d] Based on figures for 1956.
Source: UN, *Yearbook of International Trade Statistics.*

Table 4.2 *Export orientation ratio (exports as percentage of GDP)*

East Asian NICs	1950	1955	1960	1965	1970	1975	1977
Taiwan	10.5	7.6	11.7	18.3	27.0[a]/29.6	41.2	53.8
South Korea	2.3	1.9	3.4	8.6	14.3	27.6	34.8
Hong Kong	—	—	84.0	76.9	99.7	94.3	95.1
Latin American NICs	1950	1955	1960	1965	1970	1975	1977
Mexico	18.7	16.7	10.3	9.3	8.2	7.7	10.5
Colombia	14.8[b]	13.6	15.6	11.4	14.2	15.1	17.4
Chile	10.2	9.3	13.8	14.0	16.0	19.8	17.3
Brazil	6.7	8.8	6.1	7.4	6.6	7.4	7.8

[a] Based on figures for 1969.
[b] Based on figures for 1953.
Source: UN, *Yearbook of International Trade Statistics*; UN, *Yearbook of National Accounts Statistics.*

relatively unlimited international markets. This reallocation led not only to a relative but also to an absolute decline in the agricultural labour force. Labour-intensive export industries made it possible for the first time for the large labour surpluses to be absorbed. In little more than a decade, this labour surplus had been exhausted in both countries, as shown by nearly constant unskilled wages giving way to rapidly rising ones.

This recorded shift to export-substitution required a change in government policies. To enable domestic industries to compete effectively in international markets, the degree of protection was reduced, exchange rates and interest rates were maintained at more realistic levels, and efforts were made to improve the usually depressed terms of domestic agriculture. In Taiwan and South Korea, this also involved direct government action, including the establishment of export-processing zones and the rebating of import duties on raw materials used by export industries, to help ease the transition. In addition, foreign aid was initially useful in ensuring the success of government reforms, although the rapid improvement in the economic climate, including a drastic reduction in the rate of inflation, encouraged increasing levels of domestic savings and foreign investment.

During the export-substitution phase growth rates were high in both South Korea and Taiwan. But the labour-intensive export phase also has its limits. Once the unskilled labour surplus has been exhausted, as it was in both countries by the early 1970s, with the advent of an actual labour shortage real wages begin to rise steadily. Industrial output and competitive exports tend therefore to become more skilled-labour-, technology- and capital-intensive. Thus, since the mid-1970s, Taiwan and South Korea have moved into the second phase of import- and export-substitution. They began producing previously imported capital goods, processed raw materials and durable consumer articles, at first for the domestic market, but very soon after for the international market since the new type of industrial production favoured greater economies of scale while the domestic market for these goods was still relatively small. As the economies of Taiwan and South Korea have become increasingly geared to industrial production, their agricultural sectors have shrunk, becoming mere appendages to the rest of the economy.

Growth rates in Taiwan and South Korea have continued to be very high during the past thirty years (Table 4.3). Yet equally impressive is the success of these countries in reducing unemployment and improving the distribution of income.

The improvement in income distribution – measured by the income share of the bottom 20 per cent of households (Table 4.4) – has been outstanding

Table 4.3 *Annual real per capita GNP growth rates (percentage per annum)*

East Asian NICs	1950	1955	1960	1965	1970	1975	1977
	←——PIS——→ ←——PES——→ ←—— SIS SES ——→						
Taiwan	5.7ᵃ	2.8	5.1	6.2	5.7	8.3	
South Korea	4.5ᵇ	1.5	3.2	7.5	7.1	9.5	
Hong Kong	—	—	9.5ᶜ	5.8	3.8	12.0	
Singapore	—	—	2.4	7.1	18.6	5.8	
Latin American NICs	←——PIS——→ ←—— SIS ——→ ←——EP ——————→						
Mexico	3.1	2.7	3.4	3.4	2.1	−1.0ᵈ	
Colombia	3.0	1.7	1.4	3.0	3.3	—	
Chile	3.3	1.6	2.5	2.0	−2.4	8.6	
Brazil	2.8	6.2	1.6	4.5	7.4	3.8	

ᵃ Based on figures for 1951–5.   PIS = Primary Import Substitution.
ᵇ Based on figures for 1953–5.   PES = Primary Export Substitution.
ᶜ Based on figures for 1963–5.   SIS = Secondary Import Substitution.
ᵈ Based on figures for 1975–6.   SES = Secondary Export Substitution.
                                 EP = Export Promotion.
Source: Calculated from indices in UN, *Statistical Yearbook* (1978, United Nations Publication Sales No. E/F xvii.1, and other years); for Taiwan, calculated from IMF, *International Financial Statistics Yearbook* (Washington, D.C., 1979).

in comparison with other developing countries. In fact, it is not really surprising that income distribution improved after the mid-1970s. Once the labour surplus has been fully absorbed by labour-intensive industry during the export-substitution phase, it is usual for wages to rise and industrial output to become less unskilled-labour-intensive. This is supported both by the evidence of LDC development in general and by the rather crude analysis associated with Simon Kuznets' inverse U-shaped hypothesis.[3] What is more surprising is that, in both South Korea and Taiwan, the distribution of income seems actually to have improved during the period of most rapid early growth, contrary to the experience of other developing countries as well as to the Kuznets hypothesis.

It is possible to establish a link between the way growth is generated and the way income is distributed.[4] One of the most important determinants of the distribution of income among households (size distribution) is the distribution between different types of income, including wage, property and 'merged' agricultural income (functional distribution). The functional

Table 4.4 *Income share of the bottom 20 per cent of households (percentages)*

East Asian NICs	1950	1955	1960	1965	1970	1975	1978
Taiwan	—	2.9[a]	5.0[b]	7.8[c]	8.8[d]	—	—
South Korea	—	—	—	8.2[c]	7.5[f]	—	—
Hong Kong	—	—	—	—	5.6[g]	—	—

Latin American NICs	1950	1955	1960	1965	1970	1975	1978
Mexico	—	—	3.9[h]	3.7[i]	4.2	—	—
Colombia	—	—	5.0[j]	3.0[c]	3.2	—	—
Chile	—	—	—	—	4.8[k]	—	—
Brazil	—	—	3.0	—	2.7	—	—

[a] Based on figures for 1953.   [g] Based on figures for 1971.
[b] Based on figures for 1959–61.   [h] Based on figures for 1963.
[c] Based on figures for 1964.   [i] Based on figures for 1967–8
[d] Based on figures for 1972.   [j] Based on figures for 1962.
[e] Based on figures for 1966–8.   [k] Based on figures for 1968.
[f] Based on figures for 1969–71.

Source: S. Jain, *Size Distribution of Income: A Compilation of Data* (Washington, D.C., 1975); Korea 1975: H. Choo, 'Probable Size Distribution of Income in Korea: Over Time and By Sectors', in 1977 CAMS-IER Seminar; Taiwan 1975: C. Chen, 'Over Time Changes of Personal Income Distribution in Taiwan (1964–1974)' in 1977 CAMS-IER Seminar; and *World Development Review* tables.

distribution depends in turn on the use made of different factors of production in the development process in the context of a surplus labour situation. For example, if the product mix and the technologies used are increasingly labour-intensive, the share of labour income will usually increase. It follows from this that, because labour income is usually more evenly distributed than total income, the overall distribution of income will improve during labour-intensive industrialization. The size distribution also depends on changes in the distribution of particular types of income, the distribution of skills and physical assets between families, and the rate at which the reallocation of families between more or less equitable sectors of the economy takes place. In countries with a substantial agricultural sector, such as Korea and Taiwan, it is also helpful to distinguish between rural and urban households as differences in economic activity result in corresponding differences in income distribution.

During the 1960s, Taiwan and South Korea achieved not only very high growth rates but also high and rising levels of income equality due to the unusually high share of labour in national income and also to the rapid absorption of surplus unskilled labour into rural and urban industries during the course of the decade. During the 1950s and 1960s, the distribution of rural families' agricultural income also improved, first as earlier land reforms began to take effect, and later as new technologies were introduced. Innovations included a more intensive use of land through double cropping and the shift to more labour-intensive crops such as mushroom and asparagus, in place of the more land-intensive rice and sugar crops, which particularly benefited poorer farmers with small holdings.

Poor and landless rural families in East Asia, especially Taiwan, also benefited from the decentralized nature of industrialization. The development of rural industries meant that the share of total rural family income provided by industry increased from around 30 per cent at the beginning of the export-substitution phase to around 50 per cent by the time it ended in the early 1970s, with even higher percentages for smaller, poorer farmers and previously underemployed agricultural workers. Because rural non-agricultural income was even more equitably distributed than agricultural income, the overall equity of rural family income improved considerably during the 1960s and early 1970s. Moreover, rural industries were increasingly labour-intensive throughout the period, as shown by the high and rising share of labour in total rural income. Finally, the relaxation of controls on, for instance, domestic credit, foreign exchange, and the importation of raw materials, including fertilizer, prevented the continued discrimination against small-scale and rural enterprises common to other developing countries.

Though perhaps less spectacular than urban growth, balanced growth in the rural sector was an essential feature of the East Asian countries' successful economic development. Rural industries were able to offer extra employment and higher incomes to traditional farmers and agricultural workers, and the reduced costs of urbanization more than offset the loss of economies of scale that would have resulted from a more centralized process of industrialization. It is also true that the presence of a modern rural industry contributed to the modernization of agriculture, both by acting as an incentive 'window' and by making new technology and inputs readily accessible to farmers.

In the urban sector, where virtually all family income is generated by manufacturing and service industries, labour's share in total income was high in the initial import- and export-substitution phases, rising from an already impressive 50 per cent in the early 1950s to about 60 per cent by 1975, while in other developing countries, including the Latin American NICs, it has remained at about 40 per cent. So even in the relatively capital-intensive urban sector, the East Asian NICs, in recognition of their comparative advantage in unskilled labour, chose a more labour-intensive method of production and mix of products than is usual. The exceptionally high and rising share of urban income *before* the labour surplus was exhausted is contrary to the predictions of both Simon Kuznets and Arthur Lewis[5] and was a very important factor contributing to the overall equity of the distribution of income, especially in Taiwan.

During import-substitution the usual disbursement of windfall profits, by means of import-licensing, overvalued exchange rates and preferential interest rates acts as a disincentive to the efficient choice of products and processes. In the absence of adequate pressure to become efficient, domestic industries have little motive to thoroughly investigate the range of technologies on offer from abroad, or, more importantly, to undertake the local research and development necessary to adapt these technologies, as well as the choice of products, to local conditions. The choice of options is sometimes restricted by the simple lack of information, and sometimes by such institutional barriers as 'tying' by aid donors or by multinational salesmen. Patents and licensing systems may also limit the number of technologies and products from which local industry can choose.

In East Asia, from the early 1960s onward, policy reforms liberalized credit and foreign-exchange markets, reduced protection and thus encouraged and facilitated domestic producers in their search to compete successfully in foreign markets. The pattern of labour-intensive growth that emerged, balanced between urban industry, rural industry and agriculture, and based on import-replacement rather than simple imitation, was successful in rapidly generating employment until unskilled-labour-shortage conditions were reached by the end of the decade. The East Asian economies, in other words, successfully graduated from a rent-seeking society during the import-substituting 1950s to an efficiency-seeking society during the export-substituting 1960s.

III

The Latin American countries are far too dissimilar for us to be able to establish a Latin American 'type'. Even among the so-called NICs of Latin America it is hard to discover the strong resemblance that exists among the East Asian NICs (or, for example, the countries of sub-Saharan Africa).

Nevertheless, there are important general differences between, on the one hand, Korea and Taiwan, and, on the other, say, Colombia, Chile and Mexico, which must be borne in mind in any discussion of the broader relevance or irrelevance of the East Asian development pattern.

The features which distinguish the Latin American from the East Asian NICs include an earlier commencement of industrialization, a lower population density, more plentiful natural resources, a higher initial per capita income, a less equitable distribution of assets, a larger size, and, possibly, somewhat weaker human resources, in terms of a lower level of literacy and fewer skilled entrepreneurs.

Nevertheless, the earlier colonial experience of the Latin American NICs can be said to have been similar to that of Korea and Taiwan. On the whole, they exported land-based minerals or tropical cash crops to pay for imports of industrial consumer goods. And, as in East Asia, they later embarked on a strategy of import-substituting industrialization, probably towards the end of the nineteenth century (although some observers argue that it was not seriously initiated until the depression of the 1930s). Again, traditional export revenues were used to finance the emergence of new industries, which produced non-durable consumer goods in place of previous imports.

Growth rates in the Latin American NICs during the import-substitution phase were almost as high as in the East Asian countries, largely because of their natural advantages, including an abundance of raw materials, and their higher initial per capita incomes. But in Latin America the policies which accompanied import-substitution were generally more extreme than in East Asia, in part because the strategy persisted so much longer. One consequence of this was a much greater neglect of the food-producing agricultural sector, reinforcing the damage done earlier by the Spanish and Portuguese colonialists, who had largely ignored the agricultural sector in favour of the more lucrative business of mineral extraction. In both the Latin American and East Asian NICs, governments assisted the emergence of a new industrial elite from the old landowning and commercial elites by erecting protective barriers and ensuring windfall profits. The difference between them lies in the precise tools that were used to support import-substitution, in their severity, and in their duration.

The difference is best illustrated by the contrasting paths taken at the end of the initial import-substitution period. The Latin American NICs, faced, as in East Asia, with a declining rate of industrial growth and the threat of price wars in the protected domestic market, as early as the 1930s but certainly by the end of the 1950s decided to continue import-substitution but by shifting to the manufacture of producer and durable consumer goods, at first for the domestic market but after 1970 for export as well. This might at first glance appear to resemble the stage of more capital-intensive import- and export-substitution that began in East Asia in the 1970s; the crucial difference is that the Latin American NICs moved *directly* from the first stage of import-substitution to the production of more sophisticated, skilled-labour-, capital- and technology-intensive goods instead of *first* exhausting their labour surplus by means of an export-substitution phase. This strategy demanded an even greater degree of protection than before. Thus, while at the end of the initial import-substitution period protection was gradually reduced in East Asia, it was intensified in Latin America. (In the mid-1960s, for example, Korea had negative rates of effective protection on non-durable consumer goods, Brazil rates of 50–60 per cent.) Real interest rates remained low, if not negative; the agricultural sector's terms of trade continued to be depressed; and the neglect of the food-producing agricultural sector worsened, so that even countries traditionally self-sufficient in, or exporters of, food became net food-importers.

As a consequence, the East Asian NICs have restructured their economies far more towards exports (from 10 to 60 per cent of GDP over the past 30 years) than the Latin American NICs (from 10 to 15 per cent). Moreover, exports of manufactured goods have risen to a much higher proportion of total exports in the East Asian NICs (e.g. from 10 to 90 per cent in Taiwan compared with from 10 to 25 per cent in Mexico). Since the 1970s, however, even the Latin American NICs have substantially increased their export of non-traditional, manufactured, goods in response to the still low levels of domestic demand. Part of the increase has admittedly been in non-durable consumer goods, especially textiles, shoes and gloves. But most of it has been in higher-technology-, capital-intensive products such as cars, aircraft and electrical machinery.

This has taken place not because the Latin American NICs have been able to produce these goods competitively, but because such exports are now generally (even by Prebisch and his followers) recognized as a sign of successful development which governments are willing to subsidize. A much smaller percentage of Latin American than East Asian total manufactured exports are consequently directed to advanced industrial markets where they would presumably be best able to compete on the basis of lower labour costs.

In Latin America, therefore, the production and export of mainly capital- and technology-intensive products was promoted at the end of 'easy' import-substitution, while in East Asia labour-intensive export-substitution followed *prior* to the more capital-intensive import- and export-substitution phase. The Latin American path did not require an overall change in policy. Whereas in East Asia governments reduced protection and encouraged market forces, Latin American governments could continue to select certain industries and firms for direct support in the form of tax rebates, preferential loans, and export subsidies, or by assuring private firms of continued high windfall profits in protected domestic markets in exchange for meeting rising export targets with internal (to the firm) subsidization.

The Latin American NICs were able to finance this prolonged period of import-substitution coupled, later, with export promotion – as well as to pay for an ever larger volume of food imports – by relying on their plentiful natural resources and, increasingly, their ability to attract foreign loans. But while the Latin American NICs were able, until recently, to maintain very respectable growth rates, their development strategy has been, for some time, socially costly. By skipping the initial labour-intensive export-substitution phase, and by moving instead straight to the capital-intensive import-substitution phase (with export promotion eventually added), the Latin American NICs achieved far less favourable employment and income-distribution levels than was the case in East Asia. Moreover, they laid the basis for the debt and growth crisis which has overtaken them in the last few years.

In the Latin American agricultural sectors, the initially worse distribution of land and the continuing relative shift towards primary export crops and away from food crops as import-substitution was maintained resulted in a lower labour-intensity and a less favourable distribution of agricultural incomes than in East Asia. The process of industrialization was also more centralized, i.e. rural non-agricultural income constituted a far smaller share of total rural family income. In Colombia, for instance, non-agricultural rural income's share has fallen from 15 per cent to 10 per cent during the past 30 years compared with a rise from 30 per cent to more than 50 per cent in Taiwan. Moreover, rural industries and services have been much more capital-intensive and have therefore contributed much less than in East Asia to improving the overall level of employment and the distribution of income. Finally, urban labour's share in total urban income has been much smaller – and has fallen steadily - over virtually the entire period. Given their initially higher levels of per capita income and smaller labour surpluses, the Latin American NICs would have needed a shorter period of labour-intensive export-substitution. Instead they tried to 'skip' the phase altogether and thus failed to mobilize the remaining pockets of unskilled labour in the development process.

What made it possible for the Latin American countries to nevertheless maintain high growth rates, even after 1973, was their ability to export raw materials and secure foreign capital inflow. Since 1979, however, they have run into increasing difficulties, as real interest rates have risen and protectionism increased, and, in the past couple of years, as oil prices have fallen and banks have cut back their lending. Since 1980, there has been virtually no growth in Latin America; imports have been drastically reduced and an increasingly larger share of export revenues is needed merely to service previously incurred debt.

The East Asian countries, on the other hand, have been able to maintain healthy growth rates. Both Taiwan and South Korea have thus far avoided serious debt problems. Since the early 1960s, Taiwan has not relied heavily on foreign borrowing, public or private, to finance its economic development; Korea has borrowed a great deal more, but, because its export performance has been consistently better than that of the Latin American countries, its debt has not reached unmanageable proportions. Both East Asian countries have shown a good deal of resilience in response to the worsening international environment of the 1980s, i.e. exports have continued to rise, albeit more slowly.

Contrary to popular belief, the East Asian NICs have enjoyed no special advantages in securing access for their industrial exports into US or other Western markets. In fact, the evidence suggests that whenever they have threatened troubled domestic industries, Western countries have retaliated by imposing 'voluntary' quota arrangements from which less successful or laggard countries, such as Indonesia, have remained exempt. It is worth noting, however, that once a country has reached the stage where it is able to compete successfully in international markets, it is likely to have acquired sufficient skill and flexibility to overcome many obstacles, including the defensive measures resorted to by the advanced industrial countries.

In theory, of course, a country should be better, not worse, off if it has an abundance of raw materials and access to foreign capital, in that additional resources should help ease the pains of policy adjustment. In practice, however, such 'advantages' may also be used to put off, or entirely avoid, such difficult policy changes. In the Latin American NICs decades of import-substitution have led to deeply entrenched habits and the emergence of powerful groups, including industrialists, organized labour and the civil service, with a vested interest in resisting reform or even fairly moderate changes in policy. Plentiful natural resources plus foreign capital, while they may ensure higher growth rates, also lead to an excessively 'strong' exchange rate which prevents labour-intensive exports from breaking into the international market. But plentiful raw materials and the easy availability of foreign capital also create a more important psychological barrier to policy change in that a country assumes it can 'afford' to continue import-substitution as it moves into ever more expensive and capital-intensive areas of production and export. The East Asian NICs (and at an earlier stage Japan) did not have the same easy alternatives as the Latin American NICs but were forced to stay more in step with their changing long-run comparative advantage.

IV

The Latin American countries can, of course, still move towards a more competitive export pattern and a more balanced domestic growth pattern, if they want to. A phase of labour-intensive industrialization may be essential – if only for a short period – to relieve unemployment and improve income distribution as well as to enable some of these countries to learn to compete effectively in international markets. The export of natural resources is likely to remain an important source of revenue in the long term, but balanced domestic growth, i.e. more productivity increase in domestic agriculture, will be likely to play a more important part in Latin American development than was the case in East Asia, not only because their domestic markets are larger but also because demand in the developed world is likely to be a relatively greater problem in the years ahead. By focusing mainly on the achievement of balanced domestic growth and, to a lesser extent, on developing a competitive export sector, the Latin American NICs can reduce their dependence on trade but without resorting to the usual costly protectionist measures. Even though the East Asian countries are smaller and thus have to rely more on exports, their ability to integrate export production into a vigorous balanced domestic economy has been crucial to their success in adjusting to domestic and external shocks during the 1970s and early 1980s.

It would be technically fairly simple for the Latin American countries to move gradually from selective export promotion to more general export-substitution. The problem of overvalued exchange rates, brought about by natural-resources export strength, which prevents industrial exports from entering world markets, can be addressed by monetary/fiscal policies and/or accumulating reserves abroad to try to sterilize the inflows. Minimum wage legislation can be postponed and union power kept in check until the remaining labour surplus has been exhausted. Most important, the rural sector can be made more productive, by improving its basic infrastructure, by undertaking the necessary research and development, and, more generally, by the central government adopting a less paternalistic attitude, especially towards local government, and fully recognizing the vital role it has to play in the course of successful development.

Latin American governments may, however, find it politically difficult to change course. Industrialists, for example, will be reluctant to exchange windfall profits in low-volume/high-margin domestic markets for earned income in high-volume/low-margin export markets. Nor will trade unionists be eager to accept lower wages in exchange for higher labour incomes, or civil servants a dismantling of controls which give them power. Those who lose most under the present system – the unemployed and underemployed in both the urban slums and the rural areas, as well as the medium, small-scale and would-be entrepreneurs – have relatively little influence on policy. Yet the scale of the present crisis may well force a change on Latin American governments. It should be noted that even the East Asian governments, generally considered tougher and brooking less opposition from relatively weaker trade unions and industrial interests, initially also found it politically difficult to abandon import-substitution and delayed introducing reforms for a number of years, until it became clearly impossible to maintain the strategy. Necessity, not superior wisdom, proved the mother of invention.

When the East Asian NICs did reform their systems, foreign capital was indeed useful in easing the adjustment. In the same way, the West can now play a vital role in assisting the Latin American NICs to introduce politically sensitive reforms – should they want to – by making additional loans contingent upon a commitment to long-term structural adjustment. In the past, despite all the talk of a need to restructure debtor economies, Latin America's creditors have preferred to concentrate on immediate debt repayment issues. Yet, in their own self-interest, commercial banks, financial institutions and donor countries should view multilateral discussions with Third World countries as a way to identify and correct the underlying developmental problems that have contributed to the present financial crisis. Such discussions could take place in an independent forum – along the lines of a country-focused Pearson Commission World Development Council – rather than appearing to serve the interests of any particular financing agency. Although there is a danger that both the donor and Latin American governments will prefer to conduct business as usual, the present crisis also provides an opportunity to tackle Latin America's underlying problems and thus simultaneously to ensure the stability of the international financial system.

In the real world, economies are, of course, far too complex to be divided into the distinct groups or well defined stages of development that have been used here to underscore the analysis. Yet the greater subtlety or 'greyness' of the real world also suggests that economies are sufficiently adaptable to change course at a given time. No development pattern is inevitable or irreversible, and there have indeed been important exceptions to the general trends in both East Asia and Latin America. South Korea, for example, is in many respects strikingly different from Taiwan and has much in common with some of the Latin American NICs, especially Brazil. Since the 1970s, when export targets were set and governments began putting pressure on individual firms to meet them, we have witnessed a partial return to import-substitution-cum-export-promotion, such as in the area of the petrochemical industries. Moreover, Korea's relative neglect of the agricultural sector, reversed only recently, meant that it had to rely more heavily (than Taiwan) on foreign capital; it has in the past borrowed more than ten times as much both to support rapid industrial expansion and to pay for food imports. Brazil, on the other hand, went in for a good deal of labour-intensive export-substitution, especially between 1963 and 1973, in the form of occasional bursts of exports of non-durable consumer goods such as textiles and shoes, in addition to its overall strategy of more capital-intensive import-substitution-cum export-promotion. There are also strong indications that Brazil is now putting greater emphasis on the achievement of balanced domestic growth, in particular by increasing food production for domestic consumption relative to the production of primary cash crops for export. Colombia and the Southern Cone countries have attempted partial export-substitution packages in the recent past. And even Mexico had made some tentative progress towards trade liberalization and reform of its agricultural sector until it was interrupted by the oil boom.

Any attempt to establish the 'ideal' development strategy for a particular country must obviously take into account local conditions as well as the state of the world economy. The relative importance of a labour-intensive export-substitution phase will depend upon such varying factors as a country's size, population density, resource endowment, per capita income and wage structure. The scope for export-substitution will also be determined by the level of world demand. It is likely, however, that if the Latin American countries decided to undertake a major restructuring of their policies, they would achieve the flexibility to cope with increasing Western protectionism as well as other unanticipated exogenous shocks. Their relatively smaller labour surpluses and higher per capita incomes would, in any case, mean that a short period of labour-intensive export-substitution would be required. It would indeed be presumptuous as well as misleading to suggest that the policies followed in the past by the East Asian countries should now be adopted wholesale in the Latin American context. Nevertheless, a comparison of the economic performance of both the East Asian and Latin American NICs would seem to demonstrate fairly convincingly that more growth can be achieved via – rather than in spite of – an equitable, employment-intensive development path, and that the present debt crisis can perhaps yet be converted into an opportunity to address some fundamental structural issues. But this can only be done on a country-by-country basis with all the interested parties, most of all the country's own planners and decision-makers, participating and agreeing on the substance of required reforms.

NOTES

1 It is assumed here that in the course of transition to economic maturity, an economy passes through a number of phases, each with its own distinctive structural characteristics, *modus operandi*, and associated policies. This is not to imply that any development path is 'inevitable' but simply to record what seems to have occurred in the four East Asian countries (and, at an earlier stage, Japan).

2 It is worth noting that Korea's less favourable initial conditions and subsequent agricultural policies resulted in lower levels and rates of increase of agricultural productivity, causing in turn an initially higher and faster-growing need for food imports.

3 The inverse U-shaped curve hypothesis states that as a country's per capita income improves over time, income distribution deteriorates until it reaches a minimum level – corresponding to the exhaustion of the labour surplus – beyond which income distribution improves with further increases in per capita income. (See S. Kuznets, 'Economic Growth and Income Inequality', *American Economic Review* (March 1955).)

4 See J. Fei, G. Ranis and S. Kuo, *Growth With Equity: The Taiwan Case* (Oxford, 1979).

5 S. Kuznets, *op. cit.* W. A. Lewis, 'Economic Development with Unlimited Supplies of Labour', *The Manchester School* (May 1954).

PART TWO

Case Studies

5 Brazil's Foreign Debt: The National Debate

JULIAN M. CHACEL

The aim of this chapter is to describe and analyse the national debate which has surrounded the problems created by Brazil's huge debt. In fact, it is a sequel of an earlier presentation made at Chatham House last April, to which some updating has been added. The speed of events, in a country such as Brazil, makes updating a necessity. Since April 1982 the external accounts situation has experienced a significant deterioration. Negotiations with private foreign banks are stalled, waiting for an IMF reappraisal of the adjustment programme of the economy and the resumption of its financing to Brazil. Payments due to the Bank for International Settlements were suspended. Time is running short and the country is on the verge of default.

Nevertheless, I have tried to present here a dispassionate report on the diversity of views and have chosen to make a rather descriptive presentation. Interaction between economics and politics is strongly suggested, while on the other hand, in view of the required synthetic character of the present chapter, the tangle of economic relationships must be kept in mind as background to the whole subject matter.

1. At the end of 1983 the foreign debt of Latin America amounted to $300 billion. Slightly less than one-third of this sum corresponds to Brazil's share – undoubtedly, the lion's share. Looking into the process of acceleration of foreign indebtedness that took place during the period 1973–83, one can identify as the origin of that process the first oil shock and the strategy that followed in order to carry out the inevitable structural adjustment which was required in the case of a country highly dependent upon oil imports.[1] Contrary to most industrialized economies, Brazil rejected from the outset the admission of recession as the path to adjustment. Within the strategy context, the heavy call on foreign loans had two purposes: to finance investments and to generate working capital.

A vast investment programme focused on import substitution of raw materials and capital goods was launched early in 1974. For several years, the physical level of oil imports was kept fairly constant, in spite of the sharp price increase. Looking back, one cannot avoid the feeling that the strategy which was adopted was largely based on the expectation of recovery of the world economy within the maturation time required by the investment programme – an assumption beyond the control of Brazil's national will. To say the least, it was a dangerous gamble, a risky bet.

Through abundant supplier's credit accompanied by 'free' financial loans, a bridge was built between investment funds and working capital provided by external savings.

Some investment projects were submitted to sharp criticism both in terms of size and priority. This is particularly so in the case of huge steel mills, a railroad for transporting iron ore, and, most of all, the nuclear power plants programme. Although energy oriented the priority granted to nuclear energy in the Brazil–German agreement, it was fiercely questioned by significant sectors of society on the grounds that there were untouched hydraulic resources of more than 200 MW. Nevertheless, there is no doubt that the productive capacity of the Brazilian economy has substantially increased[2] and is able to give a quick response to a surge of world trade.

2. The numerical progression of the foreign debt after the first oil shock can be summarized as shown in Table 5.1.

Obviously, the aggravation of the balance-of-payments situation was heavily influenced in more recent years, after the second oil shock, by the perverse combination of an acute increase in international interest rates and a sharp decline in the terms of trade. From a chronological viewpoint, however, the turning of the tide can be dated precisely to September 1980. At that moment, monetary authorities had short-run liabilities which exceeded, for the first time, net foreign reserves, so that, whereas these reserves had been able to finance 70 per cent of imports in December 1978, this figure dropped to 13 per cent in September 1980. In the face of that empirical evidence one may ask why policy-makers were so reluctant to recognize the need for renegotiating the terms under which foreign loans had been contracted. The answer probably lies in the interaction between economics and politics. On the one hand, the idea that pervaded the minds of public officers was that world recovery was just around the corner. On the other hand, there was a feeling that going to the IMF as a precondition to start renegotiating with private banks could jeopardize the process of political liberalization which was already in effect.

3. Actually, that process had to go through direct elections for state governors scheduled to be held on 15 November 1982. The need for

Table 5.1 *Brazil's medium- and long-term external debt*[a], *1968–82*

Year (Dec.)	Gross external debt		Net external debt	
	Amount ($ million)	Annual increase (%)	Amount ($ million)	Annual increase (%)
1968	3,780	—	3,523	—
1969	4,403	16.5	3,747	6.4
1970	5,295	20.3	4,108	9.6
1971	6,622	25.1	4,899	19.3
1972	9,521	43.8	5,338	9.0
1973	12,572	32.0	6,156	15.3
1974	17,166	36.6	11,897	93.3
1975	21,171	23.3	17,131	44.0
1976	25,985	22.7	19,441	13.5
1977	32,037	23.3	24,781	27.5
1978	43,511	35.8	31,616	27.6
1979	49,904	14.7	40,215	27.2
1980	53,848	7.9	46,935	16.7
1981	61,411	14.0	53,904	14.8
1982	70,197	14.3	66,203	22.8
1983[b]	75,131	—	—	—

[a] Excludes short-term debt. Official figures show a total external debt in December of 1982 of the order of $83.3 billion.
[b] March 1983.
Source: Banco Central do Brasil.

reaching that landmark with safety certainly prevented monetary authorities from having recourse sooner to the IMF, notwithstanding the fact that the alarm bell had been sounded two years earlier. It is worth mentioning the emotion with which a large proportion of Brazilian society views the role performed by the IMF. The origin of this mistrust, which goes back to the late 1950s, was the dramatic break-up of negotiations by President Kubitschek on the grounds that the Fund insisted upon an orthodoxy that would be detrimental to the need for fast economic development. Since then the image of the IMF, in many Brazilian minds, ranging from business to politics and the academic, is that of an international organization which is manipulated by the leading economies of the world. Therefore, the conditions set up by the IMF to provide help to less developed economies which are in trouble are on the basis of restraining aggregate demand and imposing an austerity programme leading necessarily to recession in societies that are already stricken by structural unemployment. In short, unacceptable strings are attached, which represent in some sort a surrender of national sovereignty.

Therefore, calling on the Fund prior to the aforementioned elections would have been a risky step, to the extent that if adroitly exploited by the opposition as a national issue, it could have led it to a sweeping victory, the implication of such a victory being an electoral college hostile to the incumbent administration and the disruption of the political liberalization timetable.

Putting the political argument aside, now that the electoral gap has been overcome, some outstanding members of the Congress recognize that the main role of the IMF, which is much more important than that of providing financial help, is to serve as external auditors and global viewers of the state of the economy, on behalf of a solvency programme that could be the basis for renegotiations with both private banks and creditor governments. If a less emotional criticism could still be made of the IMF, it would be that the present world is quite different from what it was 40 years ago, in the aftermath of the Bretton Woods Conference. In other words, an international institution designed to deal with fixed exchange rates and temporary imbalance of payments cannot cope, nowadays, with world problems emerging from structural balance-of-payments difficulties and floating exchange rates. Facing a plurality of structural imbalances, the IMF financial strength would be largely inadequate and its adjustment strategy, calling for prolonged recession in several economies simultaneously, would be considered an antiquated way of thinking.

4. The agreement recycled between the Brazilian authorities and the IMF, at the beginning of 1983, envisaged three basic points: a $6 billion surplus in the balance of trade, a significant reduction of the public-sector deficit by cutting investment and eliminating subsidies to credit and final consumption, and the parity of the exchange rate taking into account the rhythm of domestic inflation as compared with external price movements. In assessing the performance of Brazil after the agreement, IMF officials objected to the behaviour of the public-sector deficit and the agreed-upon financial scheme was temporarily suspended. From the Brazilian viewpoint, that breach of the agreement was explained by a maxi-devaluation of the exchange rate, which was enforced after the signature of the agreement. The 30 per cent devaluation placed an additional burden upon the financing of state-owned companies, in terms of national currency. Moreover, the conceptual framework of national accounting and macroeconomic relationships used by IMF economists did not make room for the peculiari-

ties of a widely index-linked economy such as Brazil's. Therefore, the accceleration of inflation spurred by the maxi-devaluation brought about a problem in measuring out the public-sector deficit owing to different accounting approaches, with IMF officials continuing to measure the public-sector deficit in terms of stock, and the Brazilian monetary authorities stressing that the need for financing on an annual basis should be accounted for in terms of flow. By using the index-linked value of treasury bonds as reference, those technical differences were finally resolved and a new agreement drawn up, which is now awaiting approval by the IMF Board of Directors.

5. Rescheduling and renegotiating a foreign debt of the size of Brazil's is obviously a rather complex task. Over 80 per cent of that debt is made up of liabilities against the international money market involving more than 1,100 American, European and Japanese financial institutions. Difficulties of coordination and harmonization of conflicting interests constitute, to say the least, an administration's nightmare. In such a context, it is not an easy undertaking to evaluate the scheme for renegotiation of foreign debt which began to be implemented after December 1982, backed up by a group of leading American commercial banks. However, some comments may be proffered on the basis of the proposal which was set forth by Brazilian authorities at the meeting that took place at the Plaza Hotel in New York.

The official estimate then established about the total needs for external capital in 1983 is summarized in Table 5.2.

6. Facing a collapse of international reserves, Brazil's monetary authorities were forced to present a comprehensive plan for refinancing its external accounts in 1983, divided into four so-called 'projects': (a) new loans to the amount of $4.4 billion to be granted by foreign commercial banks in proportion to their share in the pre-existing debt; (b) automatic renewal of $4 billion due to be amortized during the year;[3] (c) preservation of short-term commercial credit lines estimated by the Central Bank to be of the order of $8.8 billion; and finally, (d) restoration of $10 billion of inter-bank credit lines for Brazilian banks abroad.

Leaving aside projects c and d, the capital needs would be of approximately $15 billion, to be covered as follows: $5.6 billion coming from commercial banks, $4.5 billion in medium- and long-term loans, $2.2 billion from withdrawals from the IMF, $2 billion in direct investment and inter-company loans, and $0.4 billion in short-term credits.

The proposal became a source of sharp criticism even within Brazil. To begin with, it had the implicit assumption of $6 billion surplus in the balance of trade, to be obtained from a $2 billion increase in exports and a

Table 5.2 *Gross long-term borrowing needs from foreign banks (in $ billion)*

	1982	1983
Requirements	19.0	16.8
Current-account deficit	14.5	6.9
Amortization, long-term	7.8	7.2
Export credits granted, net	0.7	1.1
Change in gross international reserves	−4.0	1.6
Sources	19.0	16.8
Bridging operations	3.0	−3.0
Official	1.0	−1.0
Foreign banks	2.0	−2.0
IMF drawings	0.5	2.5
Project loan and supplier credits	3.1	4.5
Direct private investment	1.1	1.5
Other, net	0.5	0.0
Inter-company loans, gross (law 4131)	0.8	0.5
Brazilian commercial banks	0.9	0.6
Short-term credit lines	−1.8	0.6
Financial institutions	−1.8	NA
Non-financial institutions	NA	0.6[a]
Foreign commercial banks (long-term)	10.9	9.6
Reinvestment of amortization due	4.2	4.0
Commitments made in 1982 for drawing in 1983	NA	1.2
New long-term funds to be contracted	6.7	4.4

[a] To replace decline of bank short-term lines that occurred in late 1982 with new lines from non-financial entities.
Source: 'The Brazilian Strategy in the Recent Financial Crisis', address by Carlos Geraldo Langoni, Governor of the Central Bank of Brazil, 20 December 1982, New York.

decline of over $3 billion (30 per cent reduction) in imports. In view of the constant demand of Brazil's domestic production for imports of foreign goods, a severe reduction of imports would mean deepening recession through the appearance of new bottlenecks. Moreover, there was marked scepticism about the very figures of the proposed scheme. Not only was the amount envisaged for project d considered to be of doubtful implementation, but project a was considered to be insufficient in the light of prospects concerning the chances for total approval of projects b and c. Some projections were considered to be too optimistic, as in the case of direct investment, the estimate of which was based upon a 50 per cent increase, in spite of the gloomy domestic-investment climate.[4] Even if the proposed plan were totally successful in its four basic points, it would not be able to restore minimal safety conditions for the management of Brazilian external accounts. Starting from a rather weak position of foreign reserves (some non-convertible assets included), a $1 billion increase would not make a significant change in the precarious international liquidity situation.

Considering that a major part of new foreign resources would be engaged in the liquidation of 'bridge-loans' granted by the US Treasury and the Bank for International Settlements, by the end of 1983 Brazil would continue to be in an extremely vulnerable position as far as foreign exchange is concerned.

In mid-1983 the sentiment taking shape among several segments of Brazilian society, including politicians, entrepreneurs, academics and the military, was that the renegotiation of the country's foreign indebtedness should encompass several years ahead and a partial suspension of the payment of interest. According to those groups, this would be the only way to allow the country to have a breathing-space in order to pull itself together and prevent default.

The national controversy that is going on about how the foreign debt problem should be dealt with seems to forget that five times during the present century Brazil has negotiated an international moratorium. Early in the 1900s the first funding loan was obtained and payment of principal and interest suspended. Another moratorium was declared at the outset of World War I. During the period of the Vargas dictatorship, payments were suspended in 1931–2; in 1934 a partial agreement that reduced debt service from £24 million (sterling) to £8 million was obtained. From 1937 to 1940 payments were totally interrupted and only resumed in March 1940. More recently, partial renegotiations of the foreign debt took place in 1962 and 1964. Finally, in December 1982, a new renegotiation with the international private banking system started, the outcome of which may lead again to a moratorium.

The different opinions are polarized between the preference for a 'unilateral' moratorium and the absolute need for reaching a solution through negotiation.

It must be said that, from either a legal or semantic standpoint, there is not in the Portuguese language a concept such as 'unilateral' moratorium. The moratorium concept is a delay which is *granted* by creditors to debtors, and which may or may not change other contractual conditions. It follows that a moratorium is always the outcome of a process of negotiation. What

75

the supporters of the idea of a 'unilateral' moratorium are really suggesting is the temporary suspension of payments that are due to the rest of the world, without the consent of creditor countries. In other words, a call for default. Some adherents of this line of action go even further and suggest the creation of a 'debtors' club' involving Argentina and Mexico, aiming, through a coalition, at the consolidation of a position of strength, explained by the compounded sum of the debt of these three countries in terms of the total Third World indebtedness. However, and these are the points of view of government officials and people on the other side of the spectrum, to break relations with the international financial community would not imply the end of recession to the extent that the slump is produced by external-accounts strangulation. On the contrary, it will deepen and prolong the downward movement of domestic economic activity. Those who call for a 'unilateral' moratorium are making the false assumption that the breaking of external negotiations would not affect the balance-of-trade surplus.

When they claim that starting from unilaterally suspending payment of interests, the surplus-of-trade accounts exceeding the services-balance deficit would largely allow the country to maintain its import flow paid for by exports, they seem to forget basic differences in balance-of-payments concepts. The error in this reasoning is that between accrual balance and balance of payments lies a difference of accounting in terms of physical movements of goods and services and cash flow. The trade balance should be considered under the cash-flow approach, that is, the entry and exit of foreign exchange. It must be remembered that Brazilian imports are not paid for upon arrival, but generally financed at six months' term. On the other hand, pre-export financing lines (project c) allow that exports that would only be delivered several months later can produce an immediate entry of foreign exchange. Therefore, it is obvious that a 'unilateral' moratorium would mean the cessation of import and export credit lines, and more pressure on the availability of foreign exchange, which in turn would aggravate instead of alleviate internal recession.

7. Sooner or later the problem of Brazil's external indebtedness will have to be solved. The solution which will be worked out will certainly have a political content. There are several arguments pointing in that direction. First, the responsibility shared by lenders and borrowers in building up Brazil's foreign debt. It is a well-known fact that, historically, lenders tend to be less cautious towards borrowers in a context of high liquidity and easy money. From that angle, private commercial banks failed to watch the behaviour of the terms of trade of countries like Brazil, and the ratio of

export to import prices is a significant indicator of the capacity of repayment.[5] The banks, however, did not take into account Brazil's capacity to repay the loans, and continued to grant new loans and raise the spread. Secondly, in the event of a formal renegotiation, a revision of grace periods and a rescheduling of periods of maturity are essential to give borrowers objective conditions for the fulfilment of their international obligations. Without a recovery of world trade, improvement in the terms of trade and less protectionism in creditor countries, such objective conditions will not be met. For the developing countries, increasing barter trade is just a second best within the foreign-exchange constraint and will not supply the necessary excess of trade earnings needed in order to ensure repayment. Thirdly, the external-trade strangulation (import side) will result in prolonging and deepening recession, with the risk of bringing political destabilization in the largest and most populous country in South America. Someone has already said that street riots in São Paulo may be the fuse which will detonate the collapse of the international private banking system. Since it is obvious that lenders cannot change conditions under which financial funds have been tapped, it follows that the problem posed by the indebtedness of newly industrializing countries cannot and will not be solved without the intervention of the treasuries and central banks of creditor countries. In the same context, it is worth noticing that without negotiations encompassing governments and international agencies, the scheme considered by commercial banks is not workable at all. Under the conditions that still prevail, Brazil's net financing transfer in 1983 will amount to something between $1.5 and $2 billion. Therefore, the recent call, made by Brazilian ministers, on the Paris Club, is a step that goes beyond the search for symmetry; it aims to involve European governments in a process which has already been started with the US authorities.

8. Among the several sectors of the Brazilian society, there is a growing realization that it would be impossible for the country to meet its financial responsibilities without a new approach to the problem of foreign indebtedness. In fact, the debt service represented, just a few years ago, less than 50 per cent of export earnings: now these payments absorb 100 per cent. There is less and less room for manœuvring. Moreover, it is a source of social exasperation that the international real interest rate is now roughly twice the historical rate because of deficit spending in the United States. All of which raises the feeling that, by compressing imports to a critical level, the country is being punished by a US defence policy which is basically linked to the

77

East–West confrontation and ultimately linked to the number of missiles to be installed on either side.

In fairness, it is worth mentioning that there is also a growing realization that the negotiation which was started in December 1982 was badly conducted by the Brazilian authorities. The need for new money was grossly underestimated and some basic obligations with the IMF were not fulfilled. Nevertheless, assuming that finally private banks will get the green light from the IMF in order to refinance Brazil, some doubts can be cast on the so-called 'classical' model of renegotiation. For a number of years to come Brazil will need an injection of new money which amounts to $5 billion every year. That means that, following the classical approach, Brazil will need a jumbo loan every six months. There are several obstacles involved in this approach. Jumbo loans tend to be underestimated; they are not automatically granted; they present a high profile and the burden is inequitably distributed among banks irrespective of their size and financial strength. In addition, the 'classical' model only contemplates renegotiation of the principal and maintenance of the level of short-term indebtedness. Therefore, it is imperative that a new negotiation path encompassing a partial refinancing of interests should be found. Since private banks as financial intermediates cannot suddenly change the terms under which loans have been granted, it follows that from the creditor countries' side the search for a scheme that allows interest refinancing will be a primary responsibility of the international lending agencies and governments. At this stage there is an urgent need for a political solution.

Brazilians realize that the policy of foreign indebtedness has merely postponed the implementation of an austerity programme. But nobody knows beforehand the results, in terms of less inflation and less employment, of fiscal and monetary policies aiming at compressing aggregate demand.

What everybody does know is that, in terms of stagflation and unemployment, the social fabric of Brazil will not remain intact. In that context, the balance-of-payments strangulation and the lowering of imports beyond a minimum level will play a significant role. Responsibilities must be shared by the nation and by the Western world. If not, the country will certainly be heading towards default.

It is true that, as a nation, Brazil can survive with 300,000 barrels of oil a day and with conventional technology. But the disorderly impoverishment of the country through a closed-economy model will push it again towards an authoritarian regime. And the political pendulum in South America will turn in a direction which is opposite to that of the interests of Western world geopolitics.

Postscript

Since mid-1983, when this chapter was written, a third letter of intent and a subsequent addendum were sent to the IMF and approved; an agreement was reached with the Paris Club for the rescheduling of interest and amortizations on officially guaranteed loans due in 1983 and 1984; and negotiations with the private banks were resumed. As summarized in *The Economist*,[6] Brazil's latest proposal for the international financial system includes the following main points:

A new long-term loan of $6.5 billion. Each bank is being asked to make available 11 per cent of its loans outstanding to Brazil at the end of 1982.

The rescheduling of $5.5 billion of longer-term loans falling due in 1984.

The continuation of banks' short-term trade credits at their June 1983 level of $10.3 billion.

Inter-bank loans to be maintained at their June level, $6 billion at least.

By early January 1984, about $6.3 billion of the new long-term loan seemed to have been confirmed, and it was expected that an agreement would be signed by the end of the month. However, in spite of the funds provided by the banks (to which should be added $2.5 billion of government agencies), new credits and the rescheduling of debt arranged with the Paris Club, a net financial transfer is still expected in 1984.

In this context, and given that a recession also seems inevitable in 1984, two new proposals for facing the debt problem have emerged. According to the first, debt-service payments would be limited to a given proportion of exports, the outstanding payments being automatically rescheduled. The second proposal, which is more radical, is to transform Brazil's financial debt into bonds with a low real return, which might be held or negotiated by Brazil's creditors. Thus 1984 began with the question as to whether the latest Brazilian proposal would be sufficient to re-establish a satisfactory level of foreign reserves and whether Brazil would have to request additional funds from the international financial community before the end of the year.

NOTES

1 Roughly 900,000 barrels per day in 1973.
2 According to the last industrial short-run surveys, the manufacturing sector presents, on the average, a 30 per cent idle capacity. In the case of shipbuilding and capital goods that margin rises to 50 per cent.
3 The value was later reviewed upwards to $4.7 billion in order to include $500 million due to be amortized with Brazilian banks abroad and $200 million non-specified amortization.

4 For a lengthy appraisal of these reservations see Luiz A. Corrêa do Lago, 'As contas externas do Brasil em 1982 e 1983 depois da ida ao FMI', FGV/IBRE/CEMEI, mimeo, January 1983, and Paulo Nogueira Batista Jr, 'A renegociação da Dívida Externa Brasileira', FGV/IBRE/CEMEI, mimeo, February 1983.

5 Between 1977 and 1982 Brazil's terms of trade dropped by 50 per cent. That meant that the physical amount of exports doubled in order to pay the previous amount of imports.

6 *The Economist*, 22 October 1983.

6 Mexico: Learning to Live with the Crisis

GEORGE PHILIP

The Mexican debt crisis of August–September 1982 was like so many others of the type: surprising at the time, inevitable in retrospect. The main impression which one is left with is how rapidly the crisis developed and how quickly it seems to have subsided. Yet the crisis will linger in the memory within the international financial system and, still more obviously, within Mexico itself. It may also be that its more lasting consequences will be those which at the time were least appreciated. This remains to be seen. One may begin, however, with the crisis itself.

The Mexican economy began to cause concern only in mid-1981. The first sign of trouble was a weakening in the oil market. The head of Pemex, Jorge Díaz Serrano, responded in May by ordering a cut in the oil price; this proved politically inopportune and he was forced to resign. For several more months, Mexico tried to sell its oil too dear and so lost about $1 billion in exports and government revenue. Partly for this reason, the government in mid-1981 called for a reduction in public spending. Things then seemed back under control but a new shock came in November 1981 when the government issued new estimates of the size of its debt and expected deficit for the year (1981) which were both very much higher than expected. Even so, in December the government reduced subsidies on gasoline and allowed prices to rise: and in February 1982 it devalued the peso. Again, for a short time, this seemed to be enough.

What followed between March and August 1982 is an object lesson in how far an economy can deteriorate owing to panic and financial pressure, even while the underlying position remains reasonably sound. The outbreak of the Falklands conflict in April 1982 did not help; although Mexico was conspicuously uninvolved, the conflict undoubtedly raised the fear in the minds of some bankers that 'Latin America' might create serious problems for international lenders in the years ahead. In the memorable words of one scholar, the bankers having lent like drunken sailors now began to behave like frightened rabbits. Yet this is not the whole story. Much of the pressure on the peso came from the very high outflow of currency from Mexican citizens. In the two years to the end of August 1982, some $30 billion was estimated to have left the country in this way (as against Mexico's total inter-bank debt of some $60 million by this time). To a large extent, this speculation seems to have fed mainly on itself; a rational Mexican seeing the peso come under pressure would rapidly try to move his own savings. It is true also that the political leadership was highly uncertain during this period as after February the regime sought to postpone any further austerity measures until after the elections on 4 July, and it also seemed to be undoing much of the effect of the February devaluation by its policy of wage increases. The PRI (Partido Revolucionario Institucional) was scarcely likely to suffer electoral defeat in July but stood to be embarrassed if the recent political reform unleashed a dramatically high opposition vote. In the event, the election result – giving the PRI 77 per cent of the Presidential vote – was almost ideal for the government, but the economy had paid a heavy price to secure it.

August was crisis month. The country almost ran out of foreign exchange reserves, the currency all but collapsed and the payment of principal on Mexico's foreign debt was suspended indefinitely. The IMF was called in to discuss a stand-by credit. In the first week of September the government reacted sharply. The private banks were nationalized, as were all deposits in them. The $12 billion or so held in dollars within Mexico were forcibly exchanged for pesos at the new official rate of 70 pesos per dollar (a considerable revaluation against the free market levels prevailing during August), and a preferential rate of 50 pesos per dollar was also set up, creating considerable confusion as to what could be included at which rate. Imports were, by now, falling heavily and the authorities' earlier attempts to achieve a managed reduction in growth had clearly failed: a major slump had become inevitable. Politically the government shifted determinedly, although only temporarily, to the left. Exchange controls were introduced with the bank nationalization and Mexico's most prominent radical econo-mist, Carlos Tello, was called in to run the recently nationalized financial system. It also appears that the Mexican government made a brief and unsuccessful effort to bring Brazil and Argentina into a collective mora-torium on all debts to the international banks.

Since the accession of de la Madrid in December 1982, the position has gradually stabilized. There was an agreement with the IMF (just negotiated before the López Portillo government left office) which the new regime had rigorously enforced. Imports have been squeezed back to their pre-oil boom levels while the recovery in the US economy has partially compensated for continuing weakness in the oil market. Despite a substantial fall in real wages throughout Mexico, the social costs of the recession have not spilled over into political violence on any significant scale. Some limited normalization of capital markets has taken place although it will be some considerable time before full convertibility of the peso can be restored. Efforts have also been made to regularize the position of several very large private-sector bankrupts, some of whose foreign debt has been taken over by the state through the bank nationalization of September 1982. Some compensation has now been offered for this expropriation, and the banks' non-bank assets have been offered back to the private sector. The Mexican economy remains deep in recession (GNP fell by 4.7 per cent in 1983) and its foreign debt remains extremely high, but there is now cautious optimism that the situation can be managed at any rate for several more years.

The international factors which have created such problems for almost every Latin American country are well known (and are discussed elsewhere in this volume) and will be mentioned here only briefly. They include a rapid increase in US interest rates in 1980–1 and a fall in world demand for practically every kind of export product. The biggest losers were countries which borrowed heavily to underwrite rapid expansion against the collateral of future export potential. The production potential is often there (it certainly is in Mexico) but there is little or no demand except at rock-bottom prices.

While the factors making for short-term panic and those relating to the international economy are both important, it would be wrong to ignore some long-term difficulties with the Mexican economy which were perhaps somewhat submerged in discussions of these undoubtedly more salient short-term issues. It is likely that the Mexican economy would have run into difficulty, although undoubtedly of a less dramatic kind than that which actually took place, even in a somewhat more favourable world environment. One may, indeed, reflect on the fact that after three decades of uninterrupted growth, Mexico has suffered three recessions of increasing severity in just over a decade, in 1971, 1976 and 1982.

The monetarist critique of the two previous Mexican administrations (those of Echeverría and López Portillo) has a certain superficial justification. The monetarists argue that the basic cause of the 1982 crisis was a history of increasing government deficits financed more and more by international rather than domestic borrowing.[1] It would be hard to deny some basic truth to this assertion. It is remarkable that Mexico increased its foreign debt from some $9 billion in 1970 to $22 billion in 1976 and

83

around $80 billion at the end of 1982 while at the same time (during the latter period) increasing its gross oil export income from barely $200 million in 1976 to around $14 billion per annum in the early 1980s. Moreover, the government deficit, as a percentage of GNP, rose from a negligible figure in 1970 to a high of 9 per cent in the crisis year of 1976; it fell back only slightly from this figure during 1978–80, and then increased dramatically to 11 per cent in 1981 and some 16 per cent in 1982.

This critique is valid as far as it goes, but is a description rather than an explanation. First, one wants to know why borrowing was allowed to run unchecked in this way. Secondly one needs to explain why the big private firms often managed their affairs as badly as, if not worse than, the central government. If one were to explain government policy during the period simply in terms of obvious error, it would seem strange that the same error was made in successive *sexenios* (despite the painful events of 1976) and that the private sector as a whole did not do significantly better.

There remain (at least) three further points which do not conflict directly with the orthodox version, but do take the explanation further and relate the discussion specifically to Mexico rather than simply to broad macro-economic principles. The first of these is essentially structuralist and is that supply did not respond sufficiently to the pressure of demand because some fundamental flaws were allowed to develop in Mexico's growth process. The second focuses specifically on oil, and is that oil wealth is in general terms likely to be deceptive and disappointing in its effect on oil-exporting developing countries with substantial populations. Indeed, even some developed countries have suffered the perverse effects of an export bonanza. The so-called 'Dutch disease', and the damage done to British industry by oil-related currency overvaluation during 1980–2, put matters into perspective. The third point is more specifically political. It is that since the late 1960s there has been a growing conflict between the economic achievements which the political elite has considered necessary to stabilize the Mexican system and the performance which the economy actually proved capable of sustaining.

Structuralist analysis starts from the declining performance of the agricultural sector, which became increasingly evident from the mid-1960s. Although the quantity of government spending devoted to agriculture increased considerably after 1970, this proved insufficient to regenerate any real dynamism. An overvalued exchange rate has tended to work against export agriculture while a policy of food subsidy, enforced largely through low purchasing prices offered by the state food-buying agency Conasupo, has also offset the impact of direct government spending. More 'structural' factors relating to patterns of land tenure and the historical development of the agricultural sector – too complex to treat here – were undoubtedly also involved.[2] In the 1960s Mexico was a net exporter of agricultural produce; now it is a substantial importer.

Meanwhile the process of 'deepening' import-substituting industrialization came to something of a halt around 1970. Up until then the process had moved, reasonably smoothly, from consumables to heavy consumer durable goods (in which, however, foreign companies were disproportionately involved) but there was (during the 1970s) very little subsequent progress in the development of a capital-goods industry. The manufacturing export sector, despite the favourable provisions afforded to 'in-bound' products designed for the US market, also failed to expand greatly during the 1970s. A combination of a tariff structure which discriminated against both exports and capital goods, an overvalued exchange rate (at least during 1974–6 and 1979–81) and a rapidly growing oil sector after 1976 helped to atrophy the whole industrial pattern. Neither did state enterprise, despite its increasing importance, act to change this picture substantially. Apart from the oil industry, state enterprise did little to break into export markets; there were a few small publicly owned capital-goods companies largely supplying directly to the other state concerns, but the overall picture was one in which state enterprises provided subsidised goods at a loss for the benefit of domestic industrialists and urban middle-class consumer groups.[3]

As long as this pattern persisted, genuine industrial dynamism was impossible even when total demand was growing rapidly. Growth was concentrated in the same few sectors, such as automobiles, whose propensity to import was only temporarily disguised by the boom in oil exports. Indeed some have argued that the furious pace of economic growth itself, at any rate during the 1977–81 period, worked against serious diversification. Existing markets were too profitable and expanding too quickly to give domestic entrepreneurs either the time or the inclination to move into risky new sectors. The only major private-sector company which did diversify did so by embarking on a wildly ambitious and ill-conceived programme of conglomerate purchases which led it into serious financial difficulty even before the general economic downturn of 1982. The Alfa group, the largest private-sector conglomerate in Mexico, now faces complete bankruptcy although the government is doing its best to mount some sort of rescue.[4] The private sector, too, borrowed internationally to expand across a narrow sector of the economy. (Ironically, the government's one serious attempt to cool down the oil boom, a policy of high domestic interest rates, had the effect of encouraging indiscriminate private-sector borrowing abroad and so contributed to the depth of the subsequent crisis.)

The second point relates to the impact of oil exports on the domestic economy. Mexican oil production began to increase rapidly in 1974 but the effect at first was to eliminate the country's import bill; Mexico only began to export oil in a significant way in 1978 and the economic effect was heightened by the sharp increase in international oil prices in 1978–9. Thus Mexico suffered some of the classic symptoms of an oil boom. Investment increased as a proportion of GDP; the role of the public sector expanded within an already rapidly expanding economy; the exchange rate became overvalued, damaging non-oil exports and also import-competing indus-tries not heavily protected by tariff; imports boomed, increasing as a proportion of total supply within a rapidly expanding total. Official imports nearly doubled between 1977 and 1981 and unofficial imports were also smuggled in to a considerable degree; one Mexican economist said later, with only a slight exaggeration, that the chief beneficiaries of the Mexican oil boom were to be found in Texas and California. Texan department stores advertised openly in the Mexico City press during this time. More-over there was a general condition of excess demand whose potentially inflationary consequences were suppressed by overvaluing the exchange rate and subsidising the products of state companies. (State companies in Mexico disproportionately sell directly to the public rather than to other companies.) These oil-related conditions (on balance unhealthy despite the investment boom) were reinforced by an oil-boom mentality within both the public and private sectors in which policies of 'spend, spend, spend' became the order of the day. Whatever the intellectual justification for the government's spending strategy (that keeping costs down would encourage more investment, allow scale economies to develop and thus increase efficiency),[5] the sheer psychological fact of having seemingly unlimited amounts of money for the first time was a dominant feature of the López Portillo presidency. A lot of this money also went into private pockets.

The third point is more directly political. It focuses on a problem which has already been widely recognized by economists, namely Mexico's 'fiscal crisis' or 'fiscal gap'.[6] It is generally accepted that the gradual deterioration in Mexico's public finances, visible from the later 1960s, was due to the conflict between its relatively inelastic resource base and some very pressing claims on public spending. At the root of the problem lies the openness of the Mexican economy and the ability of capitalists to transfer their funds to the United States. There is also, it may be assumed, a 'natural' preference of wealth-holders for the United States rather than Mexico, so that they will invest in Mexico only if profitability appears much better than it does in the United States. But how can such profitability be guaranteed? In order to try to attract (or rather retain) such capital, Mexican governments have refrained from seriously taxing profits and have also used public enterprise subsidies to increase the potential profitability of private-sector investments. Yet a government which must spend, but cannot easily tax, will run deficits. In the long run, there is a potential for crisis.

This underlying problem was dealt with during the *desarrollo establizador* period of 1954–70 through a determinedly conservative public fiscal policy. Modest deficits were funded through the banking system, but there was no attempt at serious taxation of profits or at embarking on ambitious public spending policies which would help to arrest the gradual decay in the PRI's patronage machine and might also reduce Mexican inequalities. Inequality tended, rather, to increase throughout this period. However, by the mid-1960s, opposition to such a strategy was beginning to be mooted. It did little for the poor, was insufficient for certain clienteles which the government still needed to satisfy and was too rigid to accommodate the effects of rapid demographic expansion and urbanization. These doubts became expressed increasingly strongly after the repression of student demonstrations in 1968. (It is noteworthy that these demonstrations came after a period in which government spending on education tended to fall in relative terms, and were followed by a period in which spending on universities increased faster than almost every other category of government spending.) After Echeverría took power, at the end of 1970, the Mexican government committed itself to an ambitious programme of social spending – to spread the benefits of economic growth more widely – while none of its other objectives or constraints were modified. This increase in spending, aggravated by the impact of world recession during 1974–6, and an obstinate refusal to devalue the peso until speculation became intolerable, helped to bring about the political and financial crisis of 1976.[7]

In retrospect, it is remarkable how the 1976–82 *sexenio* followed the pattern of the previous one. ('History always repeats itself; the first time as tragedy, the second as farce.') This time, the promise of oil appeared to show that the government had at last broken through this revenue constraint and spending moved ahead at top speed and in all directions at once. However, such was the demand from the various clienteles that even Mexico's oil wealth proved insufficient to meet it and it was supplemented by heavy borrowing. Finally the renewed appearance of heavy deficits in 1981 led to a new cycle of financial crisis, devaluation and recession. The day-to-day economic policy-makers, as in 1976, proved unable to contain the growing pressures, which were largely invisible until shortly before they became irresistible.

For a political analysis, therefore, it is necessary to separate out and discuss some of these various clienteles. Why did they exert such a pull on the Mexican government? More important for the future, are they likely to pose threats to the regime now that their demands for government spending can no longer be met?

One may begin with the capitalist class itself. There are some elements of irony and paradox here. Thus, nobody is more insistent on the virtues of a balanced budget and on fiscally orthodox remedies for economic problems than the private sector, but at the same time no group is so anxious to secure various incentives – cheap inputs, cheap loans, protection – from the state. It has been shown that one of the most important factors making for social inequality in Mexico is the very high rate of return available from interest, profit and dividends;[8] tax reform would, therefore, achieve both greater social justice and a better fiscal balance. Yet reform of this kind has been repeatedly blocked – in 1972 and during the López Portillo presidency – by fear of private-sector reaction. It is of course possible to argue that the Mexican wealthy do very well out of periodic balance-of-payments crisis, for they can get their money out of pesos relatively easily and quickly and can thus reap windfall profits when the inevitable devaluation takes place. Yet it would be unjust to suggest that local capitalists engineered the crises of 1976 or 1982; they appear to have reacted to events rather than initiating them. (The more cynical hypothesis would also have to account for the fact that private Mexican companies borrowed some $15 billion in dollars during the López Portillo presidency and so suffered heavily, in some cases terminally, from the devaluations of 1982.)

Some writers have seen this problem as structurally inherent in Mexican development[9] precisely because such a pattern of development involves the state to a very significant degree while multiplying pressures upon it. A political scientist would describe this process as one of 'overload'. However, an alternative (by no means incompatible) interpretation will be suggested here which relates to the pattern of decision-making in Mexico. Members of the political elite put a lot of emphasis on establishing personal relationships with key members of the private sector in order to promote confidence. The private sector itself is quite highly concentrated (if we exclude the informal private sector which is not seen as being of great macroeconomic significance) and also fairly tightly organized.[10] Historically the private sector has had to do battle with radical Mexican governments (notably during the 1930s) and is, for its part, very keen to keep its political connections and even, on occasion, to mobilize public opinion against a Left-wing government. These close but essentially uncertain relationships (neither the political nor the business elite can count on the unconditional loyalty of the other) are conducive to the development of conspiracy theories and other forms of mutual suspicion. They also suggest, to members of both elites, that business is best done by striking deals or offering favours and not (as in classic liberal theory) by the government standing aside and creating the conditions in which enterprise might flourish. For the private sector, a favourable climate is also created by telling the government what it wants to hear. Thus, the Mexican banks in 1979–81 deliberately underplayed their suspicions that the economy was being overheated, for fear of official retribution. On the government side, good relations with the private sector may be sought in a number of ways (e.g. public-sector subsidies, maintaining a given structure of protection, refusing to join the General Agreement on Tariffs and Trade (GATT)) which are not conducive to the development of an efficient capitalism in general nor to good macroeconomic management in particular. When, finally, the size of the budget deficit, or the inappropriate tariff structure, or the overvaluation of the exchange rate, can no longer be ignored, the whole house of cards is in danger of collapsing in a welter of recrimination as each side (sincerely) blames the other for wrecking the economy through betrayal or corruption or both. Billions of dollars meanwhile leave the country and the next government is left with the task of picking up the pieces.

A second clientele is the Mexican middle class as a whole. There is a secondary difference here between the public-sector middle class (mainly those employed within the state bureaucracy directly and in the education sector) and those employed in the private sector. In Mexico, however, the living standards of both groups have ultimately depended on government policy. Moreover, if we exclude the business sector, both groups have been the most favoured by the government's policy of public-sector subsidy. Cheap gasoline,[11] cheap food and (through the overvalued exchange rate prevailing until 1982) cheap foreign travel have been particularly noteworthy here and helped to raise middle-class living standards sharply during 1977–81. It is from this sector that any Mexican government most fears hostility; indeed the system was badly shaken by the student rebellions of 1968 which, as we have seen, moved successive governments to spend very heavily indeed on university expansion. The historic role played by the intelligentsia in the Mexican Revolution and the articulateness of the university sector may make this a particularly important constituency for any government to control.[12] Mexican regimes have also feared the con-

sequences of serious white-collar unionization (white-collar and professional workers have often proved extremely militant and effective in
other Latin American countries) while the CTM (Confederación de Traba-
jadores de Mexico) has been struggling recently to unionize bank workers as
a prelude to enrolling the rest of this sector. There can be little doubt that, at
a time when quite sharp austerity will have to be imposed upon the middle
class as a whole, there is considerable potential for militancy here.

Finally there are the poor, or the near-poor. Although social inequality in
Mexico is among the highest in Latin America, it would be wrong to
conclude from this that government policy is necessarily feeble or
ineffective. A policy of selective reward may be at least as valuable in
maintaining political control over the PRI's mass organizations as one
seeking to provide universal benefit. As Laurence Whitehead has suggested,

there are complex political structures regulating the distribution of certain resources (land, water, access to credit, jobs, licences). This political distribution system
has a vital function in the organisation and control of popular forces and it parallels
and even modifies the functioning of the open market system.[13]

It is also true that, during the last decade, there have been signs that
government spending – on education, electrification, health facilities and
the extension of social security benefit – has reached at least the majority of
the poor. It is too early for this to show in income-distribution statistics but
it will in any case be impossible for the regime to maintain this real level of
services under conditions of economic stringency.

It is important, but difficult, to separate out the extent to which pressures
to increase state spending come from within the system and how far they
come from society itself. Certainly it would be misleading to talk of the
Mexican government, in the Klondike atmosphere of 1977–81, being
'forced' to spend money. Yet it would be equally misleading to suggest that
Mexican governments can expand or contract the economy just as they (or
the bankers) wish without any constraints being imposed by the need to
maintain political stability or public order. The Mexican political elite has
often stressed the impatience of its clients and their willingness to resort to
militant tactics if they were not paid off in good time. This may be a
technique in the inter-bureaucratic battle for resources or in the mechanisms of inter-elite conflict, but pressures from below have sometimes been
known to surface. One of the reasons for such popular pressure on the
government as has existed is inflation. After nearly two decades (1954–72)
of near-stable prices, Mexico from around 1973 became a country with a
serious inflationary problem, even though during certain years inflation was
semi-successfully suppressed by government subsidies. Of course, if the

underlying cause of inflation is excessive government spending, then demands for yet more spending (on subsidies and the like) in the interest of containing inflation are always going to be self-defeating. However, this consideration does not make severe deflation any more welcome or any easier to bear.

When stripped of rhetorical exaggeration and released from false premises, there remains an underlying high demand, which in all probability will prove to be politically effective, for goods and services which the government alone can provide. It could not easily be otherwise in a country where population growth is still 2.5 per cent per annum, where the flight to the cities is continuing and where one-half of the total population is 15 or younger. The overpopulated and under-serviced urban centres will continue to expand and there is as yet little sign of the government's decentralization or deconcentration policies having much practical effect. Moreover, Mexican agriculture, already weak, may collapse without continued public support. In these crucially important respects, Mexico does not have a *laissez-faire* option.

To sum up so far, therefore, Mexico has had to cope with a world environment which, during the past ten years, has made Mexico's own growth targets more difficult to achieve. The new oil revenues acted as a countervailing factor for a time, in macroeconomic terms, at the cost of distorting the economy, but international conditions became seriously adverse during 1981–2, leading to export stagnation: the import boom continued unabated. The Mexican economy also weakened during the decade as a consequence of certain 'structural' problems, notably the stagnation of agriculture and non-oil exports and the weakness of the capital-goods industry, while pressure on government spending continued to rise. These underlying weaknesses could also in part be traced to policy mistakes, but of a longer-term nature than those fuelling the economic over-expansion of 1980–81. They were partially disguised by the rapid increase in oil revenue during the 1976–80 period, but this increase also made Mexico more dependent on the oil industry and more vulnerable to the distorting effects which an oil boom tends to produce. Despite these difficulties, the López Portillo government (like its predecessor) sought to maximize Mexico's growth rate and to satisfy all of the government's diverse clienteles through an uncontrolled expansion of government spending, on such a scale that not even the oil revenues could fully finance it. Although belated efforts were made during late 1981 and early 1982 to correct the government's fiscal course, these proved too little and too late to prevent a major financial crisis in August–September 1982, whose effect was to intensify further the degree of deflation which has had subsequently to be imposed upon the Mexican economy.

If the political economy of Mexico's inflationary boom is now fairly well documented, any judgements about the future effect of Mexico's current deflation must be more speculative. There can, at least, be no doubt that deflation is being enforced. Mexican imports in 1983 fell to an astonishing low of $7.8 billion – less than half the peak 1981 level and (when inflation is taken into account) lower than for any year since 1977. GNP fell by 4.7 per cent (7.5 per cent in per capita terms) in 1983 after stagnating in 1982. Falls in the exchange rate have led to an inflation rate of over 80 per cent in 1983 – and a real fall in living standards of perhaps 30 per cent for most Mexicans (the middle class has suffered rather more than this, the working poor rather less). Exports, meanwhile, held their course and remained at $21 billion, leaving a trade surplus of around $13 billion. In 1983 this satisfied both the IMF and the main private banks. The figures for 1984 are not quite so extreme (60 per cent inflation and roughly zero growth are expected), but there is no sign that the living standards of 1980–1 will be recovered during this decade.

In the medium term, there is some prospect of a limited economic recovery. World oil demand appears at least to have stopped contracting, and there is at least the prospect of price stability. Mexico still has abundant reserves of crude oil and could fairly easily increase its present output of 2.75 million barrels a day to a maximum of 3.3 million barrels a day should a market become available. This could add (depending on the exact price) around another $4 billion, to Mexican exports. Moreover, some of the other investments (e.g. in steel, petrochemicals and transportation) under-taken during the 1976–82 period will be coming onstream during the *sexenio*, adding something to the productive capacity of the economy. It is also hard to see how the Mexican peso could again become as overvalued as it was in 1980–1; a more realistic exchange rate will certainly have a short-term effect on highly elastic items such as tourism and border transactions and may have a more durable long-term effect on the Mexican manufacturing sector as a whole. Even so, a good deal of difficult restruc-turing will be necessary if supply is to respond to these new opportunities and if the economy is to recover the dynamism which it enjoyed during the 1950s and 1960s – the structure of tariffs will need to be changed, agriculture will need to be encouraged by a realistic system of internal pricing and the exchange rate must be kept competitive. Yet these changes will have redistributive implications and will adversely affect potentially vocal urban groups at a time when living standards are already falling.

If the long-term prospects offer some limited encouragement, the difficulties of day-to-day policy-making in the short run must be considerable. Mexico still has a very large foreign debt and (despite the successful rescheduling effort of August–September 1984) is almost certain to be locked into a never-ending series of negotiations with bankers and the IMF. There remains the prospect of a heavy rescheduling in or before 1987 – just in time to coincide with the sexenial weakening of economic policy-making which has been such a standard feature of recent Mexican politics. During all of this time there will remain a danger that a temporary financing difficulty will lead to a sudden panic among wealth-holders and to capital flight (although it is unlikely that full convertibility of the peso will be restored in the foreseeable future). It is in any case hard to see very much confidence being restored to the economy while the debt overhang is so great and the course of international interest rates, oil prices and foreign trade levels so uncertain.

Mexican policy-makers do have the advantage that private-sector spokesmen are, for the time being, too subdued by their own failures, too concerned about possible government enquiries into their own affairs and too eager to retain influence on government policy-making to want to press criticism against government policies. The first two years of a *sexenio* are, in any case, something of a honeymoon period for the incoming president. Too many people hope for favours, or fear disappointment, to want to criticize an all-powerful figure whose term has more than four years still to run. Yet the restoration of growth will require more than passive acquiescence in government policy; it will require positive demonstrations of confidence which will be all the more important if capital is to move from the old over-protected consumer areas of the economy into capital goods or into exports. For its part, the public sector will have an important part to play in reactivating the economy when the foreign-exchange position makes this possible, but the expansion of the last *sexenio* (and the nationalization of the banks) has greatly extended the role of what is now a heavily over-burdened public sector. Even if some limited denationalization takes place, the government will still face a major task in improving the quality of public-sector management. The less clientelistic and more financially correct style of the present government makes the prospect of some improvement here likely, but there will be a political price to pay.

Above all, there is the political dimension. It is no longer true (if it ever was) that Mexico is governed by a combination of machine politicians and technocrats, who could impose such policy measures as they might wish upon a passive or controlled population. Ever since 1968 the political elite has sought to move away from a policy of pure control and repression. In a country which was becoming increasingly urban, literate and politically sophisticated the elite was, at that time, faced with the choice of governing through tightened repression, directed as much against the middle class as the poor (as the Cono Sur dictatorships were to attempt during the 1970s), or alternatively opening the political process gradually in a slow development towards genuine democracy. The latter course was eventually chosen and various political reforms enacted. One result was to increase the freedom of public debate, not always unconditionally (as the fate of *Excelsior* in 1976 showed), but nevertheless far more than in the past. Another effect was to give some life to the political opposition which took over 20 per cent of the vote in the 1982 elections; since then, two small Right-wing parties have achieved unprecedented successes in local and regional elections and the PRI has become seriously worried about its failing electoral appeal. Even in 1982, fears of electoral embarrassment led the López Portillo regime to postpone necessary austerity measures and thus to increase pressure on the peso. The middle class is now far more deeply alienated and the PRI's own patronage resources are far weaker than was the case then. From now on the politics of deflation will need to be managed very carefully if events are not to escape the government's control. It is not yet clear what the political constraints on deflation (or what the deflation-imposed constraints on political reform) will turn out to be. However, in 1990 it will no longer be necessary to ask the hypothetical question (much favoured for teaching purposes) 'How would the Mexican political system survive a period of economic hardship?' By then, we shall know.

So far, at least, the de la Madrid government has made it a priority to reduce the degree of corruption within the Mexican system. Genuine moral principle may play a part here (the president is known to be personally honest and strongly religious) but there is also a calculation which seems to fall into two parts. On the one hand, there can be little doubt that the over-spending of the previous *sexenio* was partly due to this traditional part of the Mexican system. Pure graft was undoubtedly a factor (as recent revelations concerning Pemex have made clear) but there are also various forms of favouritism which are rarely so crude as the direct cash bribe but which are just as effective at committing public resources. By committing himself to a clean-up and sticking firmly to this objective, de la Madrid may not make government better, but he will certainly make it cheaper.

At a deeper level, the new government may calculate that its best chance of winning public acquiescence for unpopular economic policies is to re-establish some of the moral credibility which the system so conspicuously lost during the previous *sexenio*. If the government cannot be popular under the economic circumstances, it can at least try to be respected. However, the strategy does pose problems. Quite apart from the possibly destabilizing effect of an anti-corruption purge if it came to be directed against more senior figures than Díaz Serrano, there remains the problem of how Mexico is governed. 'I know of no General', said Obregón, 'who can withstand a broadside of 50,000 pesos.' There are many figures in the PRI apparatus who run trade unions, or peasant organizations, or state governments in a similar way.[14] If morality is to be imposed seriously, how can the political machine be operated? The political elite itself draws the distinction between those who use financial inducements to strengthen their political position, and so help to reinforce the system (which is regarded as acceptable and even admirable), and those who are simply interested in personal enrichment even at the price of bringing the system into disrepute (which is regarded as disgraceful). However, this judgement may be rather fine for Mexican public opinion as a whole and, in any case, it is not always a distinction which can easily be drawn in practice.

One may ask also whether the new morality means (as now appears less likely) that honest elections will be held at a time of economic hardship. The PRI's democratic credentials, which in the past have been ambiguous to say the least ('O Lord, give us democracy, but not yet') were in 1983 put to the test earlier and more strongly than the government wished. The result was defeat for the PRI followed by ballot-rigging; in 1984 the government has quietly been promising that the rigging would stop, but this remains to be seen.

The Mexican system still has many strengths. The myth of the Revolution (dutifully kept up, perhaps more than it should be, by the intellectual Left) has undoubted social appeal, however much matters may seem to have deteriorated since the (retrospectively) glorious days of Carranza or Cárdenas. The main non-governmental interest groups – the Church, the business elite, the universities and the US official and non-official pressure groups – have all, at different times and in different ways, made their peace with the Mexican system; they may seek the modification of policies but not to overthrow the state. The political elite itself remains relatively (even if decreasingly) coherent and united and is well organized around a very strong presidential system (in some ways this works better in bad times, when unity is at a premium, than in good, when the absence of credible 'loyal opposition' or of independent mass media denies Mexico the advantages of open debate and serious criticism). Repression, though low-key, has remained as an effectively managed part of Mexican government and the security forces remain under political control. It is likely that these strengths will see the Mexican system through the next few years. Nevertheless, in the words of the ancient Chinese curse, Mexico is now living in very interesting times.

NOTES

1. One of the leading exponents of this line of thought was Dr Redvers Opie, who was highly critical of government over-spending during the oil boom years themselves.

2. For pre-1982 treatments of Mexico's agricultural problems see M. Redclift, 'Development of Policymaking in Mexico; the SAM', ILAS Working Paper No. 5 (London, 1980); C. Luiselli, 'The Sistema Alimentario Mexicano (SAM): Elements of a Program of Accelerated Production of Basic Foodstuffs in Mexico', University of California, San Diego, Center for US–Mexican Studies, Research Report Series 22 (1982).

3. I have elaborated this in G. Philip, 'Public Enterprise in Mexico', in V. Ramanadham (ed.), *Public Enterprise in Developing Countries* (London, 1984). A more general structuralist critique has been evolved at CIDE in Mexico, from which this brief summary borrows. See for example, Wilson Peres, 'La Estructura de la Industria Estatal 1965–75', *Economía Mexicana*, no. 4 (1982), pp. 15–36.

4. For a discussion of the Alfa group's transactions during this period, see the appendix of M. E. Cordero and J. M. Quijano, 'Expansion y Estrangulamiento Financiero: 1978–81', in J. M. Quijano, *et al.* (eds.), *La Banca: Pasado y Presente* (Mexico City, 1983). It is remarkable, in retrospect, both how irresponsible some of these were and how easily Alfa could get international lenders to underwrite them.

5. These assumptions appeared in the 1980–2 national plan (the first in Mexico's history) and were also outlined by the industry Minister Oteyza, who introduced the plan in January 1979.

6. E. V. K. Fitzgerald, 'The Fiscal Crisis of the Latinamerican state', in J. F. J. Toye (ed.), *Taxation and Economic Development* (London, 1978); and, more specifically on Mexico, 'The State and Capital Accumulation in Mexico', *Journal of Latin American Studies*, 10 (1978).

7. A very interesting if not always convincing defence of the Echeverría administration's economic policies is to be found in C. Tello, *La Política Económica en México 1970–76*, Siglo XXI (Mexico City, 1976).

8. See W. Van Ginnekin, *Socio-Economic Groups and Income Distribution in Mexico* (London, 1980).

9. E. V. K. Fitzgerald, 'The State and Capital Accumulation', *Journal of Latin American Studies*, 10 (1978).

10. M. Basañez, *La Lucha por la Hegemonía en México 1968–80*, Siglo XXI (Mexico City, 1981).

11. Laura Randall, 'The Political Economy of Mexican Oil 1976–79', in J. Ladman,

D. Baldwin and E. Bergman (eds.), *U.S.–Mexico Energy Relationships* (Lexington 1981) makes the point clearly that Pemex's subsidies disproportionately favoured the comparatively well-off.

12 L. A. Whitehead, 'On the Governability of Mexico', *Bulletin of Latin American Research*, 1, no. 1 (October 1981).

13 L. A. Whitehead, 'Mexico from Bust to Boom; a Political Evaluation of the 1976–79 Stabilisation Programme', *World Development*, 8 (1980), pp. 843–64.

14 For the case of Pemex and the oil workers see G. Grayson, *The Politics of Mexican Oil* (Pittsburgh, 1981).

7   The Rise and Fall of the Chilean Economic Miracle

TIM CONGDON

Laboratory experiments are, fortunately, not possible in the social sciences. But there can be no doubt that since 1970 Chile has been a testing-ground for sharply contrasting economic theories. From September 1970 to September 1973 the Popular Unity government under President Allende attempted to create a socialist economy with extensive government ownership and control. After a violent coup in September 1973 the country was moved in quite the opposite direction when a technocratic team, acting with the full support of the ruling military junta under General Pinochet, restored private ownership in many areas and opened up the economy to new competitive forces. The members of this technocratic team were known as 'the Chicago boys' because of their sympathy for the free-market doctrines associated with the University of Chicago. Although their work affected many parts of Chilean society, the emphasis in this paper is on their efforts to liberalize the financial system. The argument will be that both the apparent success of the free-market experiment until 1981 and its breakdown in 1982 can be explained largely by the course of financial liberalization. The other most salient reform, a programme of trade liberalization which opened the Chilean economy to foreign competition, interacted with financial liberalization in important ways, but it will not be discussed in detail here.[1]

The financial liberalization should be understood as part of a reaction against a long-run tendency towards greater state interference with resource allocation. This tendency dated back to the early 1930s. The first part of this chapter describes the financial system as it was in the 1950s, 1960s and early 1970s, when the Chilean economy was increasingly dominated by government and its agencies.

Financial repression in Chile

The Chilean economy in the twenty years until 1973 suffered from seriously inadequate financial institutions, which were unable to channel resources to profitable uses in the most effective way. This weakness has been termed 'financial repression' and is to be found in many other less developed countries.[2] Its main consequence in Chile was that the ratios of financial assets and liabilities, including money, to national income were low by the standards of advanced capitalist societies. The restricted level of financial intermediation reflected a previous lack of savings and investment, and was associated with a shortage of accumulated capital. It has been estimated that gross investment between 1940 and 1965 averaged only 11 per cent of gross national product and in many years hardly covered depreciation.[3]

Financial repression was partly the result of government controls. Chile had many decades of large budget deficits until the Pinochet regime and, because of the absence of a significant domestic market in public debt, governments borrowed heavily from the central bank and from the commercial banking system. The commercial banks were forced to acquire more government paper than they would have liked, usually by being obliged to maintain excessive reserve requirements.[4] They were penalised in their competition with institutions known as *financieras*, who were not subject to such onerous regulations, but were nevertheless watched by the monetary authorities. Because of these and many other restrictions on bank lending to the private sector, and because governments prevented interest rates rising to a market-clearing level, there was a continuous excess demand for credit. This was exploited by a fringe of less reputable intermediaries who may have been financed to some extent by the banks and *financieras*. The most notorious were rural moneylenders who exploited small farmers' limited access to mainstream financial institutions. A study of their activities in the early 1960s found that they reaped positive real interest rates in a range from 27 per cent to 360 per cent per annum, almost entirely on loans of under $1,000.[5]

The constraints on private financial intermediaries reduced their efficiency and made them vulnerable to charges of failing to meet the needs of the national economy. Politicians had a good pretext for establishing state-owned and state-administered alternatives. By the early 1970s these existed in great number and variety, but two were pre-eminent. The first was CORFO, a conglomerate set up in 1939 with stakes in many nationalized industries, most of which accomplished the rare achievement of being both monopolistic and loss-making; it regularly had a financial deficit.[6] The second was the Banco del Estado, a commercial bank owned by the state but distinct from the central bank. Both CORFO and the Banco del Estado directed funds to companies not only on the basis of relative profitability, but also according to governments' most urgent political priorities. There was also a tendency for cheap loans to go to cronies or useful acquaintances in the small urban elite. Shortly after his appointment as finance minister in 1977 de Castro – who became a key figure in the financial liberalization – protested against previous abuses. He condemned the behaviour of monetary authorities who 'arbitrarily established interest rates at levels which did not even compensate for inflation' and distributed 'among their friends the scant savings generated by the public'. 'Under this system many quick fortunes were amassed by certain individuals and groups who recall those times with nostalgia.'[7]

The deficiencies of private-sector financial intermediaries stemmed from rampant inflation as well as government interference. In the 1950s and 1960s Chile had, on average, the highest inflation rate in the world. The size and frequency of price changes confused the interpretation of market signals and undermined the operation of the price mechanism. This was particularly important for companies trying to assess the true significance of a particular nominal interest rate. Because they did not know whether inflation would be 20 per cent or 40 per cent in two or three years' time, they hesitated about arranging medium- or long-term finance. The time-horizon of all business decisions shortened; large investments with extended gestation periods were not undertaken, whatever their potential profitability in the long run; and the appraisal of financial risks absorbed too much management effort. It has been estimated that in the 1950s an 'excessive proportion of executive energy – 14 to 18 per cent of their time – was devoted to financial matters, and financial operations grew inordinately at the cost of production operations'.[8] Companies, unable to obtain loans from banks or other intermediaries, had to borrow and lend between themselves in the form of trade credit. Inflation hampered the development of an efficient, privately-owned and profit-oriented financial system.

Under the Allende government financial repression intensified. Programmes of nationalization became indistinguishable from organized stealing, and respect for private property disintegrated.[9] The inflation rate, which had averaged 27.9 per cent under the previous Christian Democrat government of President Frei, was 22.1 per cent in 1971, 163.4 per cent in 1972 and 508.1 per cent in 1973. As the sphere of 'social ownership' expanded, the private financial system contracted almost to the point of extinction. At the end of 1973 outstanding peso credits by the Banco del Estado were three times larger than those granted by the rest of the banking system in its entirety.

The central problems in the financial liberalization

The new economics team which took over after 1973 was well aware that the underdevelopment of the financial system in Chile was in sharp contrast to the highly sophisticated patterns of financial intermediation found in advanced capitalist societies. More particularly, they knew that the explosive inflation rates at the end of the Allende government had made people economize on money balances, and that the ratio of the money supply to national income was extremely low not only by the standards of the industrialized West, but also in comparison with Chile's past. One of their prime aims was to raise the real money supply in the hope that the loans matching the extra deposits would finance new capital investment. McKinnon's thesis – of complementarity between the money supply and the capital stock – provided a theoretical rationale for their intentions.[10] Although the focus was on the level of real money balances, the general approach was to expand the range and size of all financial institutions serving the Chilean economy. Research by Goldsmith, which has shown that the 'financial interrelations ratio' (i.e., the ratio of financial assets to national wealth) increases with income per head, confirms the pertinence of their diagnosis. Goldsmith has claimed that

the existence of clearly different forms of financial development is doubtful. The evidence now available is more in favour of the hypothesis that there exists only one major path of financial development, a path marked by certain regularities in the course of the financial interrelations ratio, in the share of financial institutions in total financial assets, and in the position of the banking system.[11]

But the programme faced two serious difficulties. First, a large financial system relies on a stable measuring-rod of value. As Chilean economists understood very well from their experiences in the 1950s and 1960s, inflation disrupts financial planning and heightens the uncertainties faced by both borrowers and lenders. Lower inflation was therefore a precondition for successful financial liberalization and inflation can be lowered only if the rate of *nominal* money supply growth is contained. But, in order to expand the *real* money supply, it was necessary to let the nominal money supply increase by more than the price level.

So the Chicago boys were ambivalent in their attitude towards the monetary aggregates. Slow money growth was required to combat inflation, but high money growth to promote financial development. Although the conundrum can be resolved in principle by a distinction between nominal and real magnitudes, there is no doubt that in practice Chilean policy-makers became rather confused about where they were

101

going. In particular, they were unsure about the value of the equilibrium ratio of money to national income and consequently lacked clear signposts for financial targeting. It should be emphasized here that the commonplace media description of Chilean economic policy as 'monetarist' is simple-minded to the point of misrepresentation if monetarism is taken to mean the absolute primacy of money-supply control as an anti-inflationary weapon. The role of the money supply in economic policy was both more subtle and more muddled than this.

Secondly, a financial system is sustained by professional expertise, notably the knowledge and experience of lawyers, accountants and bankers. One function of this expertise is to protect property rights when command over assets is transferred from their owners to entrepreneurs and companies or, in other words, when credit is extended between people. The rapid expansion of the financial system intended in Chile should therefore have been accompanied by a substantial strengthening of credit appraisal, banking technique, accounting standards and so on. As we shall see, this was not to happen. The absence of a responsible central banking tradition was also a handicap.

The initial reforms, September 1973 to December 1977

When the Pinochet regime came to power, Chile faced an economic emergency. Price increases were accelerating and the country was unable to repay its foreign debts. Orthodox and vigorous measures were taken. The budget deficit was cut from 25 per cent of national income to virtual balance in only two years, while a big devaluation helped to shift resources from domestic consumption to the external sector.

Action on the monetary front was – at least, in theory – equally straightforward. In his October 1974 report on the public finances Cauas, the Finance Minister, said that 'the monetary policy we have been applying recognizes that there is a close relation between the rhythm of growth in the level of prices and the rate of expansion of the money supply. This recognition ... grows directly out of the observation of the dramatic Chilean experience with inflation.' In addition to this fairly mechanical quantity-theory approach, the peso was devalued repeatedly 'to avoid the deterioration of the real exchange rate' (i.e., the loss of export competitiveness). Such a deterioration was judged likely to have 'very serious effects on the balance of payments and on the allocation of resources'.[12]

The two main practical steps were the establishment of uniform reserve requirements for all banks and the freeing of interest rates. Before the reforms each bank was entitled to a certain amount of central-bank credit and, at the ruling interest rate, this was invariably less than the amount it wanted. Subsequently banks were free to bid for reserves from other banks and expand their balance sheets at will, as long as they satisfied the reserve requirements. The bidding for reserves drove up interest rates. At first the central bank placed limits on this process, but from 25 April 1975 banks were free to set interest rates at any level for transactions which matured in one year or less. Real interest rates rose to remarkable levels. In 1976 the typical interest rate per month was about 11 per cent, equivalent to an annualized 250 per cent. At the same time the inflation rate, as measured by the increase in wholesale price in the twelve months to December was 151.5 per cent, implying real rates of about 40 per cent. By early 1977 real rates were even higher. In the first quarter of 1977 the average real interest rate on bank loans was 5 per cent per month, equivalent to an annualized 80 per cent.[13]

These astronomic real rates did not hinder credit expansion or economic recovery. Output slumped by 12.9 per cent in 1975 because of a stabilization crisis resulting from the simultaneous rise in oil prices and collapse of copper prices. But it then picked up 3.5 per cent in 1976 and 9.9 per cent in 1977. Private-sector credit demand was so resilient that, despite the level of real interest rates, the money supply increased by 247 per cent in 1974, 277 per cent in 1975 and 201 per cent in 1976. The first notable deceleration occurred in 1977 when the rate of growth dropped to 124 per cent.[14]

It is difficult, looking at the numbers, to believe that Cauas' early remarks on the importance of checking monetary growth were taken very seriously. Money-supply increases of over 200 per cent a year were less than the 400 per cent recorded in 1973, but they were still extraordinarily fast. Nevertheless, inflation did slow down, perhaps because the high interest rates encouraged people to hold more bank deposits. The consumer price index, which had soared by 508.1 per cent in the twelve months to December in 1973, went up by 375.9 per cent and 340.7 per cent over the same period in 1974 and 1975, but the figures for 1976 and 1977 were more reasonable at 174.3 per cent and 63.5 per cent respectively.[15]

The extreme difficulty of applying a crude quantity-theory method encouraged the Chicago boys to consider a new approach to inflation control. The change in the tone and content of official statements was gradual. In April 1975 Cauas said that inflation should decrease 'as a result of the reduction in money creation which in turn is the product of the significant drop in public spending'. The thinking here seems to be that public spending is the ultimate cause of inflation and that money creation

103

arising from private-sector credit is blameless in the inflationary process. The idea was developed more fully in the October 1975 report on the public finances. Something termed 'the degree of liquidity in the economy' was deemed to be 'a problem'. As inflation fell, the velocity of circulation would decelerate and 'the volume of money' would be 'insufficient to finance the flow of transactions'. It followed that, 'The economy must necessarily return to operating with a normal level of liquidity under stable conditions. This means that during some period money should increase more rapidly than prices and when this occurs it is not correct to speak of excess liquidity.' In more technical and precise language, achievement of lower and more stable inflation expectations would promote the demand for real money balances, while the forces behind expansion of real money balances, such as credit to the private sector, should not be viewed with alarm. The budget deficit was the real enemy, not private-sector credit. 'Equilibrium in the fiscal sector ... will guarantee the end of the long history of inflation in Chile.'[16] Policy was consistent with this proposition. By late 1976 the budget was effectively in balance and it was to remain so for the next five years.

When de Castro became finance minister in early 1977 these themes were retained and elaborated. Inflation came to be viewed more in fiscalist than in monetary terms. Private-sector credit was blessed because of the contribution it would make to the 'monetization' of the economy. In December 1977 restraint over the monetary aggregates was more or less discarded as a technique for controlling inflation. Under the new dispensation, exchange-rate management became the fulcrum of anti-inflation policy.

The abandonment of rigorous targets for money and credit growth was logically consequent on the dilemma faced by policy-makers at the beginning of the financial liberalization. As we have seen, they wanted the financial system to expand and assume the functions of resource allocation previously performed – with inefficiency and occasional dishonesty – by government. Such expansion required that money and credit grow at a higher rate than nominal gross domestic product (GDP). There was obviously a powerful demand for bank credit from the private sector since this had persisted despite astonishing real interest rates in 1976 and 1977. The quantification of restraint over money and credit seemed, to Cauas and de Castro, tantamount to placing an explicit obstacle in the way of financial development. In their view such development was essential to the initiation of rapid economic growth led by the private sector.

By late 1977 and early 1978 much had been achieved in areas other than financial liberalization. The balance of payments had been corrected, with a small current-account surplus in 1976 followed by a deficit of 4.5 per cent of GDP in 1977, quite a normal and acceptable figure for a developing country. The major structural reform was the removal of trade barriers, including the largest unilateral reduction in tariff rates ever implemented by any country. Imports grew quickly as a result, but exports were also very dynamic. Most spectacular was the increase in non-traditional exports which rose from $71.2 million in 1973 to $818.7 million in 1978. These non-traditional exports – mainly fruit, forest products and fishmeal – benefited from resource reallocation due to trade liberalization and from the policy of a competitive exchange rate to which Cauas had stated his government's commitment in October 1974.

Financial liberalization and exchange-rate management

By the end of 1977 the Chilean authorities had curbed inflation, but at rates well in excess of 50 per cent it was still above the average for the 1950s and 1960s. As further and intensified credit restraint was ruled out because of its conflict with growth objectives, the economic team embarked on an imaginative strategy to dampen inflation expectations. The hope was that in this way the costs (in terms of lost output and employment) of further reductions in inflation would be minimized. In Chile, as in other Latin American countries, the exchange rate between the dollar and the local currency is closely watched because the public knows – from many years' unhappy experience – that it is a good advance indicator of future price increases. The idea favoured in late 1977 was to announce an advance schedule of peso devaluations against the dollar, each one being smaller than the last. The link with the dollar was intended to be an earnest of the government's anti-inflation resolve, while the gradual diminution in the size of the devaluations was supposed both to reflect and to enforce a continuing decline in the inflation rate. The devaluation schedule was set out in a small table known as the *tablita*. De Castro announced the first *tablita* in February 1978.

Of course, the *tablita* would work only if people believed that the devaluation schedule could be held. De Castro and his associates designed a relatively simple central banking model, similar to the currency-board system operated over many decades in former British and French colonies, to solve this problem. They thought that the exchange rate could be maintained at the pre-announced level if the central bank had sufficient dollars to meet any claims made on it. So the vital requirement was that the central bank's liabilities (i.e., high-powered money for the rest of the economy, known as *emisión* in Chilean terminology) should be 100 per cent covered by foreign-exchange reserves. In the past the Chilean central bank's balance sheet had looked very different. Because of budget deficits the central bank had had to lend to the government and other public-sector agencies, and because of the cosy relationships with private banks it had bought much of their paper. Its liabilities were therefore matched mostly by credit to domestic entities, not by foreign-exchange reserves. But in 'the new Chile' being forged by the Pinochet government the central bank would – so it was presumed – be able to stop all forms of domestic credit. As the budget was balanced the government would have no need for funds, while de Castro was confident that rediscounting facilities to the private banks could be withdrawn without fuss.

Two further features of the proposed currency-board model should be noted. First, although the central bank itself was to give no loans to the private sector in any form, commercial banks were left free to increase their loans to the private sector as much as they wished. They had to comply with reserve requirements, but these were being progressively relaxed. The easing of reserve requirements would allow a steady rise in the money multiplier and, as a result, a given amount of high-powered money would support an increased quantity of deposit liabilities. Secondly, the ultimate base of the financial system was the central bank's foreign-exchange holdings. It was the rise or fall of these holdings which was to determine – when all the arrangements were working smoothly – the amount of high-powered money in the economy and so the behaviour of private-sector credit and the monetary aggregates. In these circumstances the authorities welcomed the inflow of capital from abroad because it added to foreign-exchange reserves. When the new system was being organized they were enthusiastic about all forms of private-sector credit, with few hesitations or provisos, and they viewed capital inflows approvingly.[17]

The *tablita* and its accompanying machinery failed. They failed amidst an economic catastrophe almost as bad as the shambles of 1973. The system's architects have, understandably, been criticized as the main culprits in the fall of the Chilean economic miracle. But proper recognition should be paid to the virtues of the new system, particularly in the Chilean context, when it was first envisaged. The aim was to terminate the sequence of slowly diminishing devaluations by fixing the exchange rate. This aim was fulfilled. The peso was pegged at 39 to the dollar in July 1979 and de Castro declared that the rate would be maintained 'for many years'. For a country like Chile, habituated to currency turmoil, this was a step forward. It reduced business uncertainty and took the exchange rate – at least temporarily – out of the political arena. It also had the desired effect on inflation expectations. The first year of the *tablita*, 1978, saw the inflation rate fall to 30.3 per cent. If everything had turned out ideally, the central banking system had even more to commend it. The supply of high-powered money to the economy would come to depend not on domestic budgetary excesses and the associated political wrangling, but on external developments outside policy-makers' control. The scope for political interference with economic variables, which had been far too great in Chile for many decades, would be much reduced. Finally, the denial of rediscounting and other facilities to private banks would end the unfair exploitation of cheap central-bank credit about which de Castro had complained so forcefully when he was first appointed. Although the private banks would be more exposed to competition because of the increased distance between themselves and the central bank, they would also be less regulated. Their new freedom would allow them to grow swiftly, enabling Chile to escape from the financial repression which had stunted its development, particularly its private-sector development, for more than thirty years. There may seem to be something of a discrepancy between Cauas' October 1974 commitment to avoid a 'deterioration of the real exchange rate' and de Castro's July 1979 pledge that the fixed exchange rate would be held 'for many years'. But the two statements reflected a common ambition, to promote financial development by ending the extreme macroeconomic uncertainty and instability which had hindered Chile's progress for so long.

The course of financial liberalization, December 1977 to October 1981

The four years from December 1977 were very exciting for the Chilean economy. Economic growth was faster than at any time since the 1920s and living standards improved spectacularly. The increase in GDP was 8.2 per cent in 1978, 8.3 per cent in 1979, 7.5 per cent in 1980 and 5.3 per cent in 1981. Among the most vigorous sectors were the new export industries. Non-traditional exports advanced from $818.7 million in 1978 to $1,820.8 million in 1980. Inflation remained moderate by Chilean standards and, briefly, even became low by international standards. Consumer prices rose only 9.5 per cent in the twelve months to December 1981. Here, without question, was an economic miracle – or so it seemed.

As Cauas and de Castro intended, the boom was driven by private-sector credit. Between December 1977 and August 1981 bank credit to the private sector rose by over eleven times (see Table 7.1). Although prices went up by about 140 per cent in the same period the increase in real terms was almost five times, a remarkable figure for such a short space of time. The growth was most rapid in 1979 and 1980, coinciding with the phase of particularly buoyant economic activity. Credits were extended in both pesos and dollars. As Table 7.2 shows, peso and dollar loans increased at roughly similar rates. Chilean banks were unable to fund their dollar lending from domestic sources and instead had to borrow heavily abroad. Their external dollar borrowings were $248.3 million in 1978, $434.8 million in 1979, $1,465.9 million in 1980 and $2,824.8 million in 1981.

The structural composition of credit growth corresponded to the economic team's objectives. With the budgetary position so strong, the public sector was not a significant participant in the boom. Indeed, small surpluses were recorded on the government's finances in 1979, 1980 and 1981. As CORFO's miscellany of industries had been restored to profit-

Table 7.1 *Assets and liabilities of the Chilean monetary sector, 1973–81*

All figures are in millions of pesos and relate to end of period.

	Domestic credit to		Other assets	Net claims abroad	Monetary liabilities (including banks' capital and reserves)
	Public sector	Private sector			
Dec. 1973	858	59	−96	−277	544
Dec. 1977	74,340	49,654	−15,101	−19,894	108,998
Dec. 1978	117,194	114,593	−25,881	12,395	356,149
Dec. 1979	154,185	206,782	−17,212	12,395	356,149

Source: Boletín Mensual (Banco Central de Chile, Santiago), May 1980, p. 880.

	Domestic credit to				Net claims abroad	Monetary liabilities (including banks' capital and reserves)
	Public sector	Private sector	Financial sector	Other assets		
Dec. 1979	125,657	205,410	3,396	14,649	14,235	363,347
Dec. 1980	130,469	358,894	14,891	43,600	69	547,923
Aug. 1981	93,797	565,881	10,767	53,652	−61,312	662,785

The figures have been compiled on different bases over this period, with the break coming at December 1979. The table is therefore presented in two parts so as to mark where different criteria have been applied.

The totals include credit extended in both pesos and dollars. The figure in the final column is the sum of all the previous columns.

Source: Boletín Mensual, May 1980, p. 1098.

Table 7.2 *The growth of private-sector credit in Chile, 1978–81*

| | Loans to private sector by commercial banks | | | |
| | Local currency | | Dollars | |
	Amount (millions of pesos)	Change on year earlier	Amount (in $m.)	Change on year earlier
Dec. 1978	57,051	—	1,000	—
Dec. 1979	104,612	+83.4%	1,642	+64.1%
Dec. 1980	191,590	+83.1%	3,551	+116.4%

Source: Boletín Mensual (March 1981), p. 625.

| | Loans to private sector by commercial banks | | | |
| | Local currency | | Dollars | |
	Amount (millions of pesos)	Change on year earlier	Amount (in $m.)	Change on year earlier
Dec. 1980	248,231	—	3,844	—
Dec. 1981	382,627	+54.1%	6,440	+67.5%

The figures are not presented on a continuous basis over the whole period because the harmonization of regulatory arrangements for banks and *financieras* made it necessary to include *financieras* in the same category as the banks after December 1980.
Source: Boletín Mensual (March 1981), p. 625.

ability by robust management, it also was not borrowing from the banks. Bank credit to the public sector fell from 125,657 million pesos in December 1979 to 93,797 million pesos in August 1981, at the same time that credit to the private sector soared from 205,410 million pesos to 565,881 million pesos. Whereas in December 1973 the public sector's debts exceeded domestic monetary liabilities by a wide margin, in August 1981 they represented only 14.2 per cent of such liabilities. Clearly, the private sector received the overwhelming preponderance of credit during the financial liberalization. Moreover, most lending operations were conducted by private-sector entities. By August 1981 the Banco del Estado, which had largely abstained from the frenzy of new lending, was a rather neglected institution. Its proportion of domestic-currency loans had fallen to 10.7 per cent. It seemed condemned to a permanent loss of market share to aggressive competitors such as the Banco de Chile (14.1 per cent) and the Banco de Santiago (8.8 per cent).[18] Regulations were being harmonized to create parity between the banks and the *financieras* so that all credit-granting and deposit-taking businesses could be integrated, on equal terms, into one financial system.

While the commercial banks lent money at a furious pace to the private sector, the central bank tidied up its balance sheet. Domestic credit to the public and private sectors was gradually eliminated in order to meet the requirements of the currency-board blueprint. Table 7.3 shows how much progress was achieved. In December 1977 claims on the public sector were by far the largest class of assets held by the central bank. As in December 1973, they much exceeded the total amount of high-powered money. Between December 1977 and December 1979 claims on government continued to grow, but more slowly than high-powered money. The central bank was able to change 'net claims abroad' from a negative to a positive figure, establishing some reserve backing for the issue of high-powered money. After 1979 the position began to approach a genuine currency-board pattern. In February 1980 the banking system lost central-bank loan facilities and became a small net creditor on the central bank. Between April and June 1980 direct lines to the non-bank private sector were also cut off and it, too, became a net creditor.[19] De Castro had acted on his angry words in 1977, making sure that 'quick fortunes' would not be grabbed by 'certain individuals and groups' with preferential access to central-bank credit. The curtailment of credit to the public sector was a less tractable problem, but it did decline by almost a third between December 1979 and August 1981. As a result of these cut-backs in domestic credit the central bank was able to cover high-powered money fully by holdings of international reserves. Indeed, from mid-1979 onwards reserves exceeded high-powered money. In late 1980 de Castro and his team believed that they had established an automatic system for regulating credit and money, comparable to the gold standard in its invulnerability to administrative discretion and political interference.

But the events of 1982 and 1983 were to demonstrate that nothing could be taken for granted in Chilean monetary control. The financial gyrations of these two years were far from automatic; they required the exercise of much administrative discretion and prompted considerable political interference. There were several sources of trouble, but without doubt one of the most important was the fixed exchange rate. Despite Chile's relative openness to international competition because of its low tariff barriers, the inflation rate did not fall quickly to international levels after July 1979.

Table 7.3 *The balance sheet of the Banco Central de Chile*

1. Structure of central bank assets
All figures are in millions of pesos and relate to end of period.

	Domestic credit to			Other assets	Net claims abroad	Capital and reserves	High-powered money
	Public sector	Private sector	Banking sector				
Dec. 1973	723	44	9	−199	−201	−48	327
Dec. 1977	87,833	2,135	6,526	−24,221	−14,344	−20,420	37,509
Dec. 1978	110,441	9,249	7,197	−27,330	−4,905	−50,379	54,083
Dec. 1979	143,315	14,999	6,168	−6,917	43,288	−121,438	79,413

High-powered money (or *emisión*) is the sum of all the columns to the left.
Source: Boletín Mensual (May 1980), p. 880.

	Domestic credit to			Other assets	Net claims abroad	Capital and reserves	Central bank liabilities
	Public sector	Private sector	Banking sector				
Dec. 1979	120,983	10,213	17,317	−6,236	61,128	−117,572	85,833
Dec. 1980	119,989	−757	2,417	−10,478	127,063	−138,367	99,867
Aug. 1981	82,010	4,371	−7,726	−13,547	141,561	−116,384	90,285

From January 1979 central bank liabilities were separated in Chilean financial statistics into high-powered money and two other categories, excess reserves and quasi-money. There is a consequent break in the series.
Source: Boletín Mensual (December 1981), p. 2831.

2. Reserve backing for high-powered money
All figures are in millions of pesos.

	Net international reserves	High-powered money	Reserves as a percentage of high-powered money
Dec. 1977	15,323	37,509	40.9
Dec. 1978	40,699	50,379	80.8
Dec. 1979	97,227	65,321	148.8
Dec. 1980	163,667	90,097	181.7
Aug. 1981	161,207	82,232	196.0

The 'net international reserve' concept used is reserves at the central bank minus IMF position. The high-powered money definition changed over the period, but interpretation would be unaffected by using other series.
Source: Boletín Mensual, several issues.

Indeed, over the whole period of the *tablita* and the fixed rate, the real exchange rate rose substantially. Morgan Guaranty has estimated that the peso's real appreciation may have amounted to 45 per cent between early 1978 and the beginning of 1981.[20] This hampered Chilean exports in world markets and made imports artificially cheap. The distortion of relative prices inevitably affected the pattern of credit allocation, causing the 1977–81 boom to become extremely lop-sided. The growth of non-traditional exports slowed down and, after 1980, they started to decline in value terms. Money was not channelled towards investment in the tradables sector, but instead financed consumption and investment in property. Too many consumption goods were paid for by personal borrowing from abroad. So-called 'capital inflows' were squandered on French cheeses and Swiss chocolates. Of course, there was some increase in investment in plant, machinery and buildings, but it was disappointing in scale. An increasing number of Chileans began to doubt that the fixed exchange rate could be held, since there was an obvious need to correct the massive current-account deficits – of $1,971 million in 1980 and $4,814 million in 1981 – which emerged. They also wondered whether bankers and loan-sharks in the private sector were any more skilled at resource allocation than politicians and bureaucrats in the public sector.

The fixed exchange rate must take some blame for the mistakes of 1980 and 1981, but it was not the only weakness in the government's programme. The financial liberalization was, in truth, much too rapid. It must be recognized that the Chicago boys were worried about the structure of the financial sector. For example, in February 1980 Bardón, the president of the central bank, contrasted a system of *multibanca*, with several small, multi-function banks, and a system of *banca especializada*, in which each institution had a particular niche in the credit market and was insulated from competition.[21] He favoured a system of *multibanca* because it aided competition. But, in general, members of the economic team were too trustful of unhampered market forces and too sanguine about prudential aspects of the credit boom.

The quintupling of real private-sector credit was accompanied by conspicuous speculative excesses. Since the real capital stock rose by nothing like the same amount, the extra credit supported very rapid increases in asset values, particularly the price of property and land. These increases in asset values led to frenetic wheeling and dealing without any underlying economic purpose whatever. The worst offenders indulged in transactions barely distinguishable from outright theft. A typical manœuvre was for a bank executive to purchase a piece of land on his account and then arrange a loan – from his bank – for another buyer, possibly a relative, at a much higher price. One of the most common abuses was the *cartera relacionada*, the loan of money to bank subsidiaries or to personnel employed by a bank. Banks were, in effect, taking in deposits to back their managers' personal investments. A report prepared by the Superintendent of Banks and Financial Institutions in 1982 showed that loans to companies connected with owners of financial institutions averaged 15.4 per cent of assets and were often more than 20 per cent.[22] Some of the most objectionable deals were organized by two particularly large *grupos*, one headed by Javier Vial and the other by Fernando Larraín and his brother-in-law, Manuel Cruzat. Their flagship banks were, respectively, the Banco de Chile and the Banco de Santiago. At one time it had been hoped they would assume the mantle of the Banco del Estado as particularly trustworthy havens for savings. When the more convoluted antics of these and other institutions were exposed in the media, the general public was appalled.[23] Some observers regarded certain manipulations as equivalent in their vulgarity and greediness to the appropriation of public property by minor civil servants at the end of the Allende government.

The fall of the Chilean economic miracle

By the spring of 1981 de Castro realized that, largely because of bankers' misdeeds, the Chilean economy was in very serious difficulties.[24] From then on he fought a continuous battle with the *grupos* to clean up the mess. In May 1981 came the first sign of trouble, the bankruptcy of Crav, a large sugar company. Investigations into the affairs of its creditor banks revealed alarming irregularities on the part of their executives. In July 1981 de Castro pushed through a law to reform the banks, placing limits on the ratio of *carteras relacionadas* to total assets. In November eight institutions were subjected to 'intervention' or, in other words, were taken out of the hands of their managements and brought under official control. Ironically, their bad loans had to be assumed by the Banco del Estado. As a state-owned enterprise, it could absorb the losses involved.

Vial retaliated by organizing a press campaign in favour of devaluation. He knew that devaluation would have spelt humiliation for de Castro who had devised the currency-board model and made it operate, with apparent success, for over two years. The correspondence columns of *El Mercurio*, Chile's most important newspaper, became lukewarm about the fixed exchange rate. It is hard to understand what Vial and his allies hoped to achieve by organizing a campaign in favour of devaluation, since

113

devaluation would clearly be a disaster for their businesses – and it was. The rumours of an exchange-rate change certainly had a calamitous effect on the economy. To keep Chileans prepared to hold pesos, interest rates had to be maintained at high nominal rates, with the monthly cost of short-term loans about 3.5 per cent in the second half of 1981. Meanwhile, the fixed exchange rate prevented price increases and inflation was negligible. Real interest rates, which had dipped to reasonable levels in 1979 and 1980, rose once again to stratospheric figures. The growth of bank lending slowed down sharply, with credit to the private sector up by 23.3 per cent in the six months to November 1981 compared with 42.3 per cent in the previous six months. Without the usual injection of new credit, property prices started to sag – at the same time that nominal interest rates were over 50 per cent a year. Against this background any kind of property investment was hopelessly unprofitable. It was inevitable that construction activity would collapse and it should have been obvious to de Castro that measures to cut interest rates were essential to stop an economic catastrophe.[25] But de Castro was committed to the fixed exchange rate of 39 pesos to the dollar – and also to humiliating the *grupos* who had spoilt the financial liberalization.

Policy-making was in disarray. Public squabbles between members of the economic team and leading financiers were a daily occurrence, while the signposts of impending disaster were easy to read. A flight from the peso to the dollar developed in anticipation of an exchange-rate adjustment. The rapid lending growth in the mid- and late 1970s had raised the level of peso money balances from 6.5 per cent of GDP at the end of 1974 to 26.0 per cent at the end of 1981.[26] The Chilean people, who have abundant experience of devaluations, decided to protect their wealth by lowering the proportion of their assets held in peso deposits. De Castro was soon alerted to the major conceptual flaw in the currency-board model. When bank deposits are convertible into dollars, 100 per cent reserve cover for central-bank liabilities is insufficient to hold the exchange rate. Instead 100 per cent cover for all bank liabilities is needed. Chile did not have that. The reserves fell from $4,064 million in September 1981 to $3,679 million in January 1982 and $3,319 million in June 1982. Economic activity slumped as banking difficulties spread from the 'intervened' banks to others and as very high real interest rates deterred borrowing. Unemployment climbed from 8.1 per cent in July-September 1981 to 17.4 per cent in March–May 1982. As the government's popularity fell heavily, Pinochet had to act. In April 1982 de Castro, the obvious scapegoat, was obliged to resign.

But the *grupos* had not won. Their day of reckoning was soon to come. The Chilean economy, already suffering from grave internal disorders, was subjected to two external shocks in the second quarter of 1982. The first was an intensification of the international recession which, in June 1982, reduced the real price of copper to its lowest level for fifty years. The second was the decision by the international banking community to halt new loans to Latin America. The pretext for the ending of credits was the Falklands dispute, but the true reason was a surprisingly belated realization that countries like Chile cannot run current-account deficits of almost $5,000 million indefinitely.

Because of these external events, Chile was required – in a period of less than a year – to shift about 15 per cent of GDP into improving the trade balance. An economy which had been lop-sided in the satisfaction of domestic demand now had to be transformed into one biased towards meeting foreign demand. The peso was devalued by 18 per cent on 14 June, despite a pledge by Pinochet only a few days earlier that this would not happen. A run on the peso developed and the authorities had to let it float on 5 August. It depreciated by a further 30 per cent in a fortnight.

The attempt to restrain inflation by exchange-rate management was in ruins. The consumer price index, which had been stable in the first half of 1982, rose by 20 per cent in the second half. The upheaval in relative prices made necessary by the balance-of-payments correction was traumatic for the financial system. Banks were very exposed because of the preponderance of loans to domestic-market activities, such as construction and property. The devaluation enormously increased the peso cost of servicing dollar debts. The Banco de Chile, the Banco de Santiago and other errant institutions found that many customers could not repay their loans. Virtually the entire Chilean financial system was bankrupt. Loan losses exceeded – and, in some cases, were a multiple of – capital and reserves. The central bank and the Banco del Estado, as the only two solvent organizations remaining, had the thankless task of putting the private banks' affairs back into some sort of order. The privatization of credit and resource allocation, a task which had taken several years to accomplish, was reversed in only a few months. As numerous examples of financial skulduggery were revealed, the financial liberalization became a target for anger and mockery. The whole free-market experiment was stigmatized by its association in the public mind with the unedifying behaviour of a relatively small number of individuals. The Chilean economic miracle was over.

Conclusion: the need for prudential checks in financial liberalization

Although the Chilean economic miracle was wrecked by a relatively small number of people, it would be wrong to seek solace or excuse in some sort of conspiracy theory. The problem can be stated in very general terms. Chilean policy-makers wanted to stimulate private-sector expansion by financial liberalization. But no economy can accommodate a quintupling of the real stock of private-sector credit in a period of under four years. It was far too ambitious to proceed at such a rate. The central bank would have been fully justified, on prudential grounds, in warning the commercial banks to behave more responsibly before the credit boom degenerated into a sophisticated form of gambling. It is quite normal and proper for a central bank to exercise prudential supervision, by threatening sanctions against insubordinate institutions, in the advanced market economies. The appropriate moment for such action in Chile is difficult to judge, but it may have been as early as mid-1980. In June 1980 share prices were eight times higher *in real terms* than in January 1977, a ridiculous rate of appreciation which must have reflected market-rigging by the *grupos*.[27]

The quintupling of private-sector credit led to three sorts of difficulty. First, the expansion of peso loans on one side of the banks' balance sheet was matched by the expansion of peso deposits on the other. It became evident in late 1981 that the Chilean public was not willing to hold the much-increased quantity of peso deposits. The move out of the peso into the dollar was so extreme that the central bank could not maintain the fixed exchange rate, despite immaculate control over its credit to both public and private sectors. Restraint over central-bank domestic credit is not sufficient for exchange-rate stability if the demand for a currency is unstable. In Chile, where people are highly familiar with the dollar as a store of value and unit of account, and where guessing the next devaluation is almost a national pastime, the demand for pesos is extremely unstable.[28] The blow to confidence in June 1982 was so severe that, in future, it will be an even more arduous task to raise the ratio of money balances to national income, as the theories of McKinnon and Goldsmith suggest is needed if the economy is to achieve sustained growth.

Secondly, the high ratios of financial intermediation to national income found in the advanced market economies reflect the cumulation of many decades' experience and understanding. The various misdemeanours in Chile have been seen before, in the United States, Britain and elsewhere, on numerous occasions. But arrangements for preventing and curbing abuses exist. These take the form not only of regulatory bodies, but also – and perhaps more importantly – of banking routine, professional codes of conduct, business ethics and so on. Capitalist economies, despite their allegedly self-serving dynamic, may depend far more on 'implicit contracts' – involving trust and forbearance – than is commonly realized.[29] Despite its cultural homogeneity, Chile could not build up a large stock of such 'implicit contracts' in a few years. They may be essential to the full development of a financial system. There is something sad, as well as ironic, in de Castro's high-minded withdrawal of central-bank credit to the private banks, just when they were at their busiest robbing each other and the general public. 'The irresponsibility of bad businessmen is dangerous for the market system, in the same way as the irresponsibility of bureaucrats in the statist system.'[30]

Thirdly, the reliance on dollar loans from abroad as one ingredient in the credit boom was very risky. The fixed exchange rate and the currency-board model were not, in themselves, bad ideas. Undoubtedly, the real exchange-rate appreciation of 1978, 1979 and 1980 complicated the economy's evolution, but it is not clear that adjustment to the 1982 terms-of-trade deterioration would have been much smoother with a more flexible exchange-rate system. It should be emphasized that the trade deficit was eliminated *before* the June 1982 devaluation. Many British and French colonies operated currency boards successfully in the past, despite being exporters of primary commodities subject to extreme price volatility. Their practice was to build up surplus balances in the metropolitan power when the terms of trade were good and run down balances or borrow when the terms of trade were poor. But Chile was borrowing on a vast scale while the terms of trade were good. The need to rectify the balance of payments became drastic because, simultaneously, there was an adverse terms-of-trade shift and new foreign credits were stopped.

Financial liberalization is probably vital to the development of efficient market economies in Latin America. But the Chilean experience suggests that institutional reform should be conducted gradually and with circumspection. Today the country is hamstrung with debt, both internally and externally. It may recover from the mishandled liberalization attempt of 1977–82, but its legacy of financial excesses will constrain the economy for several years to come. In the words of a former senator to the Chilean congress, 'Before we begged and spent. Now we must produce and pay.'[31]

NOTES

1 See T. G. Congdon, '*Apertura* Policies in the Cone of Latin America', *The World Economy* (Trade Policy Research Centre, London), September 1982, for a more detailed analysis. Several papers on the subject appear in a special issue of *Cuadernos de Economía* (Universidad Católica, Santiago), published in August 1981.

2 R. I. McKinnon, *Money and Capital in Economic Development* (Washington, D.C., 1973) introduced the concept of financial repression. See, particularly, Chapter 6.

3 M. J. Mamalakis, *The Growth and Structure of the Chilean Economy* (New Haven, Conn., 1976), p. 298.

4 The assets qualifying as reserves would typically be government liabilities.

5 C. Nisbet, 'Interest Rates and Imperfect Competition in the Informal Credit Market of Rural Chile', *Economic Development and Cultural Change* (1967).

6 CORFO stands for Corporación de Fomento or Development Corporation.

7 S. de Castro, speech to Latin American Association of Financial Development Institutions on 29 March 1977, p. 237 of J. C. Mendez (ed.), *Chilean Economic Policy* (Santiago, 1979).

8 Mamalakis, *Growth*, p. 287.

9 Towards the end of the Frei government there were frequent seizures (or *tomas*) of state housing, built by two agencies known as MINVU and CORVI. 'The live-in maid of the director general of Planning and Budget obtained two sites, one for her ten-year-old son and another as insurance for herself. After the Allende government took power, many lower-level MINVU personnel took advantage of their access to keys and vacant CORVI or Social Security Fund living units.' P. S. Cleaves, *Bureaucratic Politics and Administration in Chile* (Berkeley and Los Angeles, 1975), p. 300.

10 McKinnon, *Money and Capital* develops this idea. See, for example, the proposition on p. 57 that 'if the desired rate of capital accumulation (and hence private savings) increases at any given level of income, the average ratio of real cash balances to income will also increase'.

11 R. W. Goldsmith, *Financial Structure and Development* (New Haven, 1969), p. 40.

12 Mendez (ed.), *Chilean Policy*, pp. 108–9 and 87.

13 The figures are taken from pp. 905–7 of Banco Central de Chile (Santiago), *Boletín Mensual*, May 1980. The calculation of the real interest rate is complicated in a period of rapidly falling inflation by the lack of an obvious reference period. The rate in the last twelve months may be quite different from the annualized rate in the latest month.

14 The figures are taken from p. 33 of Ministerio de Hacienda, *Exposición sobre el Estado de la Hacienda Pública* (Santiago, 1982). The money-supply concept under consideration in the text is narrow money, dominated by transactions balances. The changes relate to the twelve months ending in December each year.

15 *Exposición*, p. 69.

16 Mendez (ed.), *Chilean Policy*, pp. 159, 177 and 228.

17 The Chilean arrangements resembled those in colonial countries with currency boards. Another example may have been Panama where the local currency (the bilboa) circulates at par with the dollar and again has 100 per cent reserve backing. See 'The Panamanian monetary system', pp. 223–8, in H. G. Johnson, *Further Essays in Monetary Economics* (London, 1972). The theoretical underpinnings of the Chilean system were described in two articles in the central bank's *Boletín Mensual* of October 1980, 'Algunos Puntos Preferentes al Manejo Monetario en Chile' by A. Bardón and F. Bacigalupo and 'Inflación y Tipo de Cambio: Experiencia Reciente' by S. de la Cuadra.

18 *Boletín Mensual*, December 1981, p. 2839.

19 *Boletín Mensual*, March 1981, p. 619.
20 Morgan Guaranty Trust Company, *World Financial Markets*, February 1982, p. 7.
21 A. Bardón, 'Ventajas de un Sistema de Multibanca en un País Pequeño, con Mercado del Capitales en Desarollo', *Boletín Mensual*, February 1980, pp. 211–17.
22 The figures are mentioned in a talk by C. Cáceres, the president of the central bank, on 'Recent Developments in the Chilean Economy', mimeo, September 1982.
23 One example may suffice. Vial's Banco de Chile lent $300 million to the Banco Andino, registered in Panama, in order that the Banco Andino might shore up companies in which Vial was a large shareholder. This was despite legal restrictions on direct loans by the Banco de Chile to these companies, many of which were *empresas de papel* (paper enterprises). *Latin American Regional Reports, Southern Cone* (Latin American Newsletters, London), 11 March 1983, p. 7.
24 It should be pointed out that, by this stage, there were major divisions among the Chicago boys. Many former government ministers were involved in banking and thought devaluation necessary.
25 Sjastaad highlights the damage from excessive real interest rates in his assessment of the Chilean experiment. See L. A. Sjastaad, 'Failure of Economic Liberalism in the Cone of Latin America', *The World Economy* (Trade Policy Research Centre, London), March 1983, pp. 5–26. See, particularly, pp. 16–19.
26 *Exposición*, pp. 84–5. Peso money balances are taken to include private-sector money and quasi-money.
27 We see here part of the explanation for the very high real interest rates. The rates were high compared with the rate of increase in the prices of goods and services. But they were modest compared with the rate of increase in asset values. When increases in asset values gave way to decreases in late 1981, nominal rates of 3 per cent or 4 per cent a month soon generated a 1930s-style slump.
28 This point has obvious implications for the monetary approach to the balance of payments – or, at least, to the application of that approach to Latin American countries.
29 The term 'implicit contracts' is usually applied to labour markets. See pp. 89–92 of A. M. Okun, *Prices and Quantities* (Oxford, 1981). But it is also relevant to financial markets. A fascinating article, 'The Bagehot Problem', by F. Hirsch in *The Manchester School*, September 1977, argued that the existence of a lender of last resort creates moral hazard in banking, a problem which needs to be checked by restraints on competition.
30 P. Baraona, a former economics minister, in an interview in *El Mercurio*, 8 November 1981.
31 P. Ibáñez, in an article on 'Reglas del Juego', in the journal of *Escuela de Negocios de Valparaíso*, January 1983.

8 Venezuela: The Oil Boom and the Debt Crisis

RAMÓN ESCOVAR SALOM

Venezuela is not a typical Latin American country; it is that rare phenomenon, a democracy that has survived for more than a quarter of a century. But, like most Latin American countries, its history is made up of a series of civil wars, constitutions, short-lived regimes and long dictatorships. From 1935 to 1945 the country was governed by two moderate reformist regimes, which, together with a short-lived populist administration in the immediate post-war period, provided an interlude before one of Venezuela's most repressive dictatorships: that of Marcos Pérez Jiménez, which held power for the whole of the decade 1948–58.

The Venezuelan economy underwent a significant transformation in the 1920s, from being centred on agriculture to becoming an important oil producer, in fact the first oil exporter on a grand scale, even before Saudi Arabia achieved this status. Since then, oil has played an increasingly important role, not only in economic but also in political terms: it became the stabilizing factor during the last two dictatorships of the twentieth century, and also a fundamental element in consolidating the post-1958 democratic process. Venezuelan democracy would not have been able to survive without the revenues derived from oil exports, which enabled the country to support an affluent society. The Venezuelan state has acted as the distributor of wealth, and different social strata have received a share of it. In recent years, however, income distribution has favoured capital rather than labour and has tended to concentrate on the upper layers of the population.

After the 1973 oil shock, oil ceased to be the stabilizing factor it had been in the past and became a destabilizing one. The huge increases in oil prices produced an unprecedented growth of export revenues, and these were translated into an expansionary budget. But the new wealth also had the effect of creating new expectations among the population and distorting traditional consumption patterns. Public and private expenditure rose to unprecedented levels. But both government and society found it difficult to adapt and make the necessary adjustments when the equally unexpected decline in oil prices occurred. In order to keep up living standards, the easy way out was to borrow from the private financial market, which was only too willing to lend. The new indebtedness, however, was of a dangerous kind, consisting mainly of short-term credits and carrying floating interest rates. Eventually, international economic factors (the decline in the demand for oil, the rise of interest rates) combined with domestic economic factors (overvalued exchange rates, the non-competitiveness of non-oil exports, over-spending) to make it increasingly difficult to service the debt, and as a result Venezuela's international credit-worthiness and international prestige both declined.

The effects of the oil boom

The sudden increase in oil prices, which quadrupled in 1973, raised per capita income in Venezuela from $1,250 in 1973 to $2,300 by 1975, giving Venezuela the same per capita income level as Greece and Ireland. At one point, Venezuela's international reserves equalled those of all the Latin American countries put together. In nominal terms, the revenues for the few years 1976–80 exceeded revenues for the whole period 1929–73. Export revenues rose from $924 million in 1973 to $2.62 billion in 1976.

The extraordinary increase in oil prices had an almost immediate effect on the budget, which in 1973 alone increased from 14 billion bolivars to 44 billion ($3.2 billion and $10.2 billion).[1] The increase also had the effect of creating demographic disorder, for Venezuela became a focus for immigration from neighbouring Caribbean and South American countries. These circumstances favoured a more active role for the central government, which increased its paternalistic attitudes towards the economy and society, while productivity continued to decline.

The external effects of the Venezuelan boom soon became visible. In much the same way that the internal economic structure had drastically changed, so did Venezuelan foreign policy. From 1973 on, the consequences of economic affluence were translated into an aspiration to go beyond the traditional limits of Venezuelan diplomacy, previously restricted to the immediate geopolitical environment and relations within OPEC. Lack of experience in implementing a global style of foreign relations meant that the new policy was more vocal than effective, more theoretical than pragmatic. However, based as it was on the growing oil revenues, it did give the country a sense of self-reliance, a mood which was intensified by the nationalization of the oil industry in 1976.[2]

121

The oil nationalization was a bland, low-key operation, which coincided with the moderate tendencies of the electorate at the time and with other similar or parallel activities of the 1970s, such as the aspiration to become a more independent actor in international affairs. Like the new foreign policy, however, it was more vocal than effective. It did not alter Venezuela's international economic relations, nor did the nationalized industry become independent of the big oil multinationals, with which it remained linked through technology agreements. But oil nationalization did have an internal political impact. It was backed by all social and political sectors, even though it was orchestrated by the political elite, which had aimed at achieving this goal as a fundamental condition in the process of economic independence. The public at large did not fully understand the aims of nationalization, which were discussed in detail only at a high political level. It was not until the political leadership arrived at a consensus on the benefits of nationalization and turned them into a political banner that the government acted as the catalyst of a decision to nationalize.

The economic sphere was the area in which the imbalances of the oil shock were first noticed. The sudden and substantial increase in oil prices brought an atmosphere of euphoria which overwhelmed both the private and the public sector. From the end of 1972 to the end of 1975, Venezuela doubled its gross national product, trebled its tax revenues, quadrupled the inflow of foreign exchange to the Central Bank of Venezuela and quintupled its national reserves.[3] The psychology that prosperity was unlimited, and that the increase in oil prices was not only irreversible but continuous, permeated all decisions. The government set out in the Fifth National Plan an ambitious programme of industrial diversification. But it was unable (or unwilling) to curb current expenditure, which continued to increase at a rapid rate. Consumption, public and private, likewise grew excessively.

The period of abundance was short but intense. From 1973 to 1982 the nominal value of exports increased fourfold, from $4.4 billion to $18 billion. But imports increased fivefold, from $2.26 billion to $18 billion. The economist Mario García Araujo, who participated in the first round of negotiations to reschedule Venezuela's debt, noted that as early as 1978 Venezuela recorded a large deficit on its current account, and that if Khomeini's revolution in Iran had not provoked a further increase in oil prices, the crisis would have surfaced at an earlier stage.

By 1982 the international banks began to see with concern that the Venezuelan government was not taking any measures to stem the outflow of foreign exchange in order to adjust the economy to the new level of oil income. In fact, according to one official report, Venezuelan tourists in

1982 spent $2 billion abroad. For some time the exit of capital was to a certain extent encouraged by interest-rate differentials which favoured outward investment from Venezuela. There then occurred the crisis of confidence which provoked the massive flight of foreign exchange, estimated at $13 billion, in 1982.

On 18 February 1983 the government established new rules of foreign exchange, introducing exchange controls rather than resorting to devaluation. This measure proved to be partially successful, in that six months after the introduction of the exchange controls foreign reserves had risen by almost $2 billion to a total of $10.3 billion.[4]

The drop in the price of Venezuela's number one export had an immediate impact on the balance of trade and was a direct cause of the rapid and substantial deterioration of the Venezuelan situation. According to the Central Bank, government revenues for 1982 were reduced by $20 billion. This loss of financial resources was equivalent to the public sector's total income for that year and to one-fourth of GNP. Overall, the performance of the economy was disappointing: oil activities decreased 8.7 per cent and the agricultural and industrial sectors had poor growth rates, 2.6 and 1.7 per cent respectively.

By early 1982 it had become obvious that revenues would be 30 per cent less than had been expected. But the government was slow to react, and economic planning and the national budget did not make the necessary adjustments to take this decrease in revenue into account. Fiscal expenditure was maintained at previous levels. Consequently, 1982 recorded Venezuela's greatest fiscal deficit in history.

The cost of Venezuela's foreign policy

The effects of oil wealth were also felt in foreign policy. Not only was Venezuela a founding member of OPEC, but the idea of creating the organization had come from a Venezuelan, Dr Juan Pablo Pérez Alfonzo, Minister of Energy and Mines in the Betancourt administration from 1959 to 1964. He was the ideologue of the Venezuelan petroleum industry and the strategist of creating solidarity and standing among exporting countries. Hence Venezuela took a principal role in OPEC, a role which has declined in recent years because its reserves are smaller than those of Saudi Arabia and its production and exports smaller still. Since it had ceased to be the leading petroleum exporter, its leadership in the petroleum sector has also diminished. Nevertheless it remains firm in its adherence to OPEC and in its solidarity with the other producers. This moderate but firm, consistent

123

and conciliatory stance corresponds to attitudes within the country, which are fundamentally moderate, and derives from the fact that Venezuela is distant from the sharp quarrels and conflicts of the Middle East.

As noted, in the 1970s Venezuela changed the emphasis and scope of its foreign policy. The government which was elected in 1973 had a strong majority in parliament and greater legal powers than any previous administration. This paved the way for a more active role in foreign policy, which came in tandem with the great expectations created by the oil wealth and the government's desire to act in accordance with its new status. The idea of a great country which had its roots in the Humboldtian optimism of the nineteenth century acquired a new tone with the advent of petroleum. Foreign policy was placed in the most visible area of the grand projects.

Venezuela played a leading role in the North–South discussions, which got under way in Paris in 1975 and continued over several years, as well as in other initiatives connected with the new international economic order. It also took a clear position in favour of human rights, negotiations on the Panama Canal and Latin American integration. For a time foreign policy was defined as cooperation with, but not submission to, the United States, a relationship which developed normally despite the fact that during this period the petroleum industry was nationalized and Venezuela adopted a very independent attitude. Venezuela also sought links with the Western European democracies. In this context and to mitigate the impact of the higher oil prices from 1974 on, the country began its international economic cooperation projects. The figures drawn from the statistics of the Venezuelan Investment Fund, an agency created to conserve and channel the new resources and to obviate the danger of economic intoxication, speak for themselves. In 1974 the Fund approved a loan of $500 million for the Inter-American Development Bank, another of $500 million for the World Bank, another of $540 million for the IMF Petroleum Facility and $700 million each for the Central American Bank for Economic Integration and for the Caribbean Development Bank. In 1975 it made loans of $60 million to the Andean Development Corporation and $40 million to the Central American Bank for Economic Integration, as well as reaching agreement with Jamaica to buy about 400,000 tons of bauxite. These figures serve to give an idea of the sort of initiatives that were taken. They sprang not from a careful study of the circumstances but from an expensive and disorderly interpretation of international economic cooperation. Many of these credits were irrecoverable. They did not serve really useful purposes for the countries which received them, and in certain cases these gifts were diverted through the corrupt methods of the recipients.

The debt crisis

Deficits, public and private, were financed by borrowing. In the international financial centres, a certain disquiet arose when countries such as Poland and Romania began to have problems in refinancing their debts. The unease grew when the situation in Argentina and Mexico reached the verge of collapse. Up to this point Venezuela had not had any problems with its short-term borrowing.

The exact amount of Venezuela's public debt has not been disclosed and is difficult to estimate, since most of it was contracted independently of the guidelines laid down by the constitution. The Venezuelan state has never been notable for the clarity of its accounts, and the affluence which followed the rise in oil prices had the effect of obfuscating them irretrievably. In fact, it has been the creditor banks which have thrown some light on this question. In August 1983 external sources estimated Venezuela's public debt at $25.3 billion and its private debt at $6 billion. Venezuela was then hoping to reschedule $18 billion which matured in 1983 and 1984.[5]

Venezuela's debt is substantially less than Mexico's or Brazil's or other Third World countries, and Venezuela is better placed than other debtors to service its debt and fulfil its commitments. The total foreign debt corresponds to 196 per cent of exports, whereas in Brazil it is 424 per cent and in Argentina 359 per cent. As for the debt as percentage of GNP, using García Araujo's data, it is 43 per cent in Venezuela, whereas in Chile it is 90 per cent, in Mexico 61 per cent and in Argentina 53 per cent.[6] But the total amount of the debt is not, in my opinion, the most important point. What is more significant in the Venezuelan case is the 'quality' of the debt: the maturities, interest rates and general conditions on which the debt was contracted. Of the total debt outstanding to banks, 64 per cent falls due before 1985.[7] On Venezuela's capacity to repay this, García Araujo has commented: 'The debt cannot be repaid within the terms which have been agreed. The maturity profile for the public sector is inadequate. This is what imposed the necessity to refinance. Venezuela has neither the foreign reserves nor the domestic fiscal resources to meet obligations of such size within such a short term.'[8]

The outgoing government of Luis Herrera Campins tried to keep the political effects of the debt crisis under control in view of the coming elections in December 1983. The introduction of exchange controls early that year was the means both of keeping the rate of inflation down in an election year and of putting an end to an internal bureaucratic dispute between the president of the Central Bank and the Minister of Finance. The former favoured devaluation and the latter the maintenance of the exchange rate. Prior to the elections, no agreement had been reached between the executive branch, the Ministry of Finance and the Central Bank regarding the amount of the debt, or on the conditions and procedures for servicing it. Therefore the negotiations for rescheduling could not be completed before the election date – a notable failure in view of the fact that most of the debt was short-term. Moreover, it is revealing that the Finance Minister and the president of the Central Bank during the Herrera Campins government publicly debated the most important aspects of the debt, in a controversy lasting several months, and expressed opposite and contradictory opinions. This fundamental tension within the decision-making centres is a significant feature of the current Venezuelan situation.

The political aspect of the debt has been of prime importance in Venezuela. It was aggravated in November 1983 by the controversy about the amount and even the validity of part of the private-sector debt. The Left asked for a scrupulous examination, while the various business sectors pressed for the recognition of their entire debt. There were many problems between the government and the private sector regarding the approval of the preferential rate of exchange of 4.30 bolivars to the dollar for privately incurred debts; there were important discrepancies as regards the total amount of the private financial and commercial debt. Both debts, especially the latter, became the object of intense debate in the period preceding the elections of December 1983. There were internal squabbles between the Finance Minister and the president of the Central Bank owing to the latter's reluctance to help speed interest payments by the private sector.[9] The president of the Central Bank rejected an instruction from the Finance Minister to make dollars available to the private sector at the preferential rate, on the grounds that private debts had not been legally registered.

A significant element which has entered the debate about the debt is whether certain private debtors have not faked their foreign commitments in order to have access to preferential exchange rates. This discussion, centred in a government administrative office, draws attention not only to the economic chaos in Venezuela but also to a more profound and far-reaching phenomenon: corruption. During Venezuela's periods of dictatorship, corruption was restricted to those who benefited directly and personally from power. Democracy has widened the base of corruption: people at different social levels now take part in it. Curiously, corruption has

126

had a paradoxical effect: it has contributed to political stability. But the effects of affluence, which were powerful enough to undermine the traditional bases of society, will have to give way to austerity. Debt and corruption are interdependent problems. Honesty in public office is fundamental to creating policies for stabilizing the economy, and essential to restating the problem of the debt in more advantageous conditions. The international creditors and the IMF are awaiting these decisions. Stability can be accomplished without corruption.

The failure of the 'model' and the search for an alternative

An outstanding element in the analysis of the events which led to the present situation is what has been called the 'model'. Nobody has yet succeeded in defining it, and (more important, since it has now been superseded) no guidelines have been set for a new model of development.

Apparently, the centre of the discussion of the 'model' lies in the policy of import-substitution, which Venezuela adopted relatively late, long after Mexico and Argentina. It is not possible to assess the results of industrialization in Venezuela within the scope of this chapter. But it is important to mention that import-substitution was introduced in Venezuela in association with a political plan which from 1958 was identified with democracy, though the last dictatorship had accepted the principle. Industrialization took a peculiar direction, associated on the one hand with state paternalism and oil revenue, and on the other with political favouritism. As a result, industrial policy generated a variety of habits which in many respects were associated with the process of corruption. In short, the benefits of industrialization have been small. It has not succeeded for light industry and, as regards heavy industry, the large projects have been curbed by the world economic crisis and by high costs and inefficient management in state companies.

On the other hand, agrarian reform consumed large resources (15,000 bolivars, equivalent to about $3,500 million at the then rate of exchange) and produced few results. The beginning of agrarian reform coincided with the appearance of rural and urban guerrillas who, inspired by the Cuban revolution, believed that the time was ripe in the mid-1980s to sound the bells of revolution. Of course moderate reform, agreed by democratic consensus, did not have economic benefits. Its importance, rather, was of a political nature, since it cut communications between urban activists and peasants by establishing rural settlements which reduced social and political pressure. Later, large numbers of peasants without a vocation for the land, or without adequate or efficient state support, migrated to the cities, where they aggravated the classic Latin American syndrome of urban unrest. It should not be forgotten, however, that agrarian reform and agriculture in Venezuela, like industrialization, absorbed huge amounts of money.

Immense sums were directed to agriculture, beside those which went to agrarian reform, which often ended up financing simple as well as complex undertakings. Consequently, it was principally in real-estate speculation that large fortunes were amassed, not only under the dictatorships but also under democracy. Land suitable for building and construction, which is an industry that does not require complex management, were the great sources of private enrichment and of the so-called prosperity of the country. With regard to construction, favourable treatment, in the form of state contracts, has been given to small groups of the population, who promptly took a significant part of income and acquired political influence.

The Venezuelan economy has been based more on speculation than on production. And in the midst of abundance the state, which theoretically has great power, is basically weak because of its organization, its weak managerial capacity, its low level of efficiency and its corruption. Hence state capitalism is not, at bottom, as powerful as it would appear from a distance.

The abundance of the 1970s in Venezuela, as in Iran and other oil-producing countries, led to the belief that what is big is beautiful and what is large is powerful. The result has been that the balance of the economy has been upset, so that the economy in general has become unmanageable.

The problems facing the incoming administration of Jaime Lusinchi seem formidable. The old model has outlived its expectations, and an alternative has to be found. What will the new model consist of? A prime necessity of any new model will be to give serious consideration to the debt problem. In the monetary field, vigorously opposed views are being expressed, according to which either a devaluation with exchange control or a maintenance of the present differentials with progressive adjustments will have to take place in 1984. Whatever the outcome, the monetary measures will have to be accompanied by a fiscal reform which will cover budget, financial policy, services and tax legislation. Certainly, this will have to lead to a major reform of the administration and the public sector.

It is worth noting that, contrary to what has been the common pattern of the rescue packages for other deeply indebted Latin American countries involving close supervision by the IMF, Venezuela has kept its distance from the IMF. Although commercial bank creditors would favour a deal between Venezuela and the IMF, it has become clear that Venezuela will not accept an IMF programme. The political costs of such a deal would almost certainly require further devaluation of the bolivar and an end to multiple exchange rates. How long Venezuela will succeed in avoiding IMF scrutiny will depend on the ability of the new Venezuelan government to apply its own economic medicine and build up its foreign reserves.

Democracy will now have to pass the test of economic discipline and economic austerity. Oil will have to keep playing a central role in Venezuela's economic future. Petróleos de Venezuela (PDVSA), the leading company in the country, on which almost the entire economy rests, will have to avoid the inefficiency which characterizes similar state companies in Latin America. It will have to face the challenge of striking the right balance between the management of petroleum production, political directions and bureaucratic pressures.

Venezuela is still an oil-rich country. The president of PDVSA has stated that at the beginning of the 21st century Venezuela will have reserves of 100,000 million barrels of oil. In the Orinoco oil belt there are reserves of more than a billion barrels, with a rate of extraction of 10 per cent. But the investment budget for the industry has been reduced by 4,000 million bolivars in 1983, and there will probably be a larger reduction in 1984.

But the future is open. The years to come will demonstrate the strength or the weakness of Venezuela's institutions. The way in which the crisis is managed will determine the destiny of a country which between internal pressure and external turbulence is trying to maintain its democratic values.

NOTES

1 The exchange rate at this time (and until the 60 per cent devaluation which took place in early 1983) was 4.30 bolivars to the dollar.
2 On Venezuela's post-oil-boom foreign policy, see R. Bond, *Contemporary Venezuela and its Role in International Affairs* (New York, 1977).
3 *El Diario de Caracas*, 6 November 1983.
4 *The Economist*, 3 September 1983.
5 *Ibid., Euromoney*, August 1982.
6 M. García Araujo, *El Diario de Caracas*, 6 November 1983.
7 *Euromoney Trade Finance Report*, February 1984.
8 M. García Araujo, *op. cit.*
9 *The Economist*, 3 September 1983.

9 World Recession and Central American Depression: Lessons from the 1930s for the 1980s[1]

VICTOR BULMER-THOMAS

Introduction

It is undeniable that the present crisis in Central America has more than an economic dimension. The latter, however, remains an important factor not only in explaining the origins of the crisis, but also in accounting for its continuation. Furthermore, the economic aspects of the crisis have received much less attention than the political and geopolitical.[2] I shall therefore concentrate primarily on economic developments in this chapter.

Although the crisis in Central America is a regional one, not all countries have been equally affected. Special factors, for example, account for the collapse of economic activity in Nicaragua in 1978 and 1979, while the precipitate decline in gross domestic product (GDP) in El Salvador after 1978 is singular to that republic.

If we abstract from the special factors, however, we may observe in Central America the unfolding of an economic depression, whose prime cause is the recession of the world economy. This depression is exacerbated in several republics by features peculiar to that country, but the underlying depression (and the trade-cycle model to which it is related) can be analysed separately.

When the trade-cycle model giving birth to the current depression is analysed, it bears a striking resemblance to the 1929 depression in Central America. Indeed, it is interesting to note that 1982 is the first year since 1932 that economic activity declined in all republics at the same time.[3] This fifty-year lag should not be taken as evidence of a Kondratieff long wave, because the trade cycle is not endogenous to Central America, but it does focus attention on the earlier depression and suggest that a comparison is justified.

Much has changed in the Central American economy[4] since the 1929

130

depression. Despite the emergence of an industrial sector, however, and the growth of urbanization, the major source of dynamism remains export agriculture. This is a function both of the openness of the economy[5] and of the high share of total exports taken by agricultural products. Thus, a trade-cycle model with elements common to both periods can be found, as well as a transmission mechanism which feeds through from the export sector to the rest of the economy.

There is an additional and more controversial reason for comparing the present economic crisis with the 1929 depression. My own researches[6] suggest that the recovery from the slump at the start of the 1930s did not have to wait upon a recovery of world commodity prices. This raises the question of whether or not the mechanisms of recovery in the 1930s are applicable to the 1980s.

The Central American economies in the 1970s

The withdrawal of Honduras from the Central American Common Market (CACM) in 1970 symbolized the end of a decade in which import-substituting industrialization (ISI) had contributed to a rapid rise in real GDP. After 1970, although intra-regional trade continued to expand (at least in value terms), its share of total Central American trade declined.

Despite this, real GDP grew rapidly for most of the 1970s, based on increased earnings from traditional exports[7] as well as the sale of non-traditional exports (agricultural and industrial) outside the region.[8] The ratio of exports to GDP rose throughout the region, increasing the vulnerability of the economy to external shocks.

The rapid growth of the 1970s was affected only slightly by the oil crisis in 1973.[9] The reason for this is that the steep rise in the price of crude oil after October 1973 was matched to some extent by the rise in the price of Central America's traditional exports, particularly sugar, bananas and coffee (see Table 9.1). Thus, the deterioration of the net barter terms of trade after 1973 was much less severe than in many developing countries, where export price movements were not so favourable.[10]

The first oil crisis, therefore, did not seriously undermine the real side of the economy, but it had a profound impact on the financial side. As a small, open economy the rate of inflation in Central America is mainly determined by dollar-import prices adjusted for tariff and exchange-rate changes.[11] With tariff changes limited to once-for-all adjustments at the start of CACM and again in 1968 (when the San José protocol was introduced) and exchange-rate stability the rule rather than the exception, the inflation rate

131

Table 9.1 *Commodity prices, 1970–84*
1980 = 100

	70	71	72	73	74	75	76	77	78	79	80	81	82	83	84[a]
Sugar[b]	12.9	15.7	25.4	33.2	103.9	71.0	40.4	28.3	23.4	33.7	100.0	58.9	29.3	29.5	14.1
Petroleum[c]	6.3	8.0	8.6	12.9	37.1	39.4	40.9	45.0	45.0	60.8	100.0	116.1	116.1	101.6	97.9
Bananas[d]	44.3	37.4	43.1	44.0	49.1	65.3	69.0	72.9	76.4	86.9	100.0	107.0	99.9	114.4	90.6
Beef[e]	47.0	48.5	53.3	72.5	57.0	47.8	57.2	54.3	77.1	104.5	100.0	89.6	86.6	88.4	78.2
Coffee[f]	33.3	28.8	32.2	39.9	42.2	41.9	91.5	150.2	104.3	112.5	100.0	83.1	90.6	85.4	94.2
Cotton[g]	30.9	36.1	38.7	66.2	69.5	56.6	82.7	76.0	76.8	82.3	100.0	89.6	77.4	89.7	80.6
Terms of trade[h]	113.1	106.1	106.0	106.2	92.3	90.7	107.7	137.1	122.4	108.5	100.0	86.1	80.2	—	—

[a] August.
[b] Caribbean (pricing-point New York).
[c] Venezuela (pricing-point Tia Juana).
[d] Latin America (pricing-point US ports).
[e] All origins (pricing-point UD ports).
[f] Other milds (pricing-point New York).
[g] Liverpool Index.
[h] Price index terms of trade. Inter-American Development Bank (IDB) estimate based on official figures and ECLA publications.
   See IDB, *Regional Report for Central America* (September 1983), p. 33.
Source: IMF, *Yearbook,* 1983 and IMF, *International Financial Statistics* (October 1984).

Table 9.2 *Central America: annual inflation rates 1970–83 (%)*

	70	71	72	73	74	75	76	77	78	79	80	81	82	83
Costa Rica	5	3	5	15	30	17	4	4	6	9	18	37	90	33
El Salvador	3	0	2	6	17	19	7	12	13	16	17	15	12	13
Guatemala	2	0	1	14	17	13	11	13	8	12	11	11	0.4	0[a]
Honduras	3	2	5	5	13	6	5	8	6	13	16	10	10	9
Nicaragua	NA	NA	NA	22	13	8	3	11	5	48	35	24	25	31

[a] April to April. Taken From Banco de Guatemala, *Boletín Estadístico* (April–June 1983).

NA = not available.

Source: IMF, *International Financial Statistics, Yearbook* (1984).

in the two decades before 1970 had been kept close to zero in Central America.[12]

At the beginning of the 1970s, import prices in dollar terms began to rise and this tendency was aggravated by the first oil crisis. The result was the acceleration of the rate of inflation in Central America to double figures (see Table 9.2).

With no previous experience of rapid inflation, but with a strong tradition of fiscal and monetary orthodoxy, policy-makers might have been expected to react through the exercise of stringent financial policies and a cut-back in public expenditure. This did not in general happen,[13] largely because the coffee boom after 1975[14] swelled government revenues and reduced the inflation-induced budget deficits.

The reasons why, in the Central American context, inflation tends to provoke a budget deficit are as follows: the main component of expenditure (current and capital) is wages and salaries and there has been a natural tendency to protect the real earnings of public employees; at the same time, in an effort to keep the inflation rate down, subsidies have been paid to firms in both the public and private sector by the central governments. The revenue side of the central government's account, however, has not exhibited the same tendency to increase, because so much income is still obtained from export duties or specific tariffs (neither of which increases in line with inflation), while the lag in collecting other forms of taxation has often been considerable.

For these reasons, the central government's budget deficit as a proportion of GDP has shown a tendency to increase throughout the 1970s (see Table 9.3). The coffee boom after 1975 had two contradictory influences on this tendency; first, it swelled government revenue in the short term,[15] thereby reducing the deficit below what it would otherwise have been, while secondly it encouraged governments to undertake grandiose investment projects, which in the longer run contributed to a veritable explosion of capital expenditure.[16]

With recycled petrodollars readily available after 1973, there was a preference for funding the expanding budget deficits with foreign sources of finance, and net capital inflows rose extremely rapidly (see Table 9.4). Indeed, the level of these flows was such that net international reserves rose in more years than they fell between 1973 and 1980.

The consequence of these increased borrowings was an explosion in the rate of increase of external indebtedness. Because so much of the borrowing

Table 9.3 *Central government budget deficit as a percentage of GDP, 1970–83*

	70	71	72	73	74	75	76	77	78	79	80	81	82	83
Costa Rica	0.6	4.7	4.2	4.1	1.7	2.7	4.8	3.0	4.3	6.6	8.2	3.6	3.0	2.7
El Salvador	0.9	0.6	1.4	0.8	1.2	1.3	0.8	2.5	2.0	0.9	6.6	8.0	7.7	5.8
Guatemala	1.3	0.8	2.4	1.8	1.3	0.3	3.7	0.7	1.2	2.6	4.7	7.3	4.0	3.9
Honduras	3.3	3.1	3.8	1.8	2.9	6.0	5.4	5.0	6.9	4.4	4.7	6.2	7.4	7.1
Nicaragua	1.3	2.4	3.2	3.3	5.3	5.7	5.7	7.1	8.1	6.6	9.0	10.4	19.5	26.8

Sources: 1970–9: Consejo Monetario Centroamericano, *Boletín Estadístico*, various years; 1980–3: Inter-American Development Bank, *Annual Report* (1984).

Table 9.4 *Central America: net balance on capital account, 1974–83 (millions of dollars)*

	74	75	76	77	78	79	80	81	82	83
Costa Rica	187.1	182.1	259.6	357.7	440.8	358.8	826.1	283.2	210.9	300.0
El Salvador	154.2	112.9	100.3	41.7	369.9	−49.1	214.5	160.5	279.1	290.4
Guatemala	87.9	180.4	242.6	241.8	398.9	224.4	−74.4	290.8	353.4	263.3
Honduras	91.9	166.0	129.7	201.6	154.1	230.8	278.0	237.6	91.5	204.3
Nicaragua	240.6	223.2	40.6	194.7	−49.0	−145.6	210.9	561.8	383.5	535.9

Source: Inter-American Development Bank, *Annual Report* (1984).

Table 9.5 *Central America: external debt outstanding, end-period, public and publicly guaranteed (including undisbursed), 1973–82 (million dollars)*

	73	75	77	78	79	80	81	82
Costa Rica	344	732	1,292	1,619	1,934	2,523	3,127	3,395
El Salvador	183	383	451	647	717	926	1,049	1,335
Guatemala	206	268	625	745	820	1,050	1,384	1,510
Honduras	215	449	810	977	1,269	1,716	1,956	2,044
Nicaragua	497	823	1,108	1,199	1,417	2,145	2,639	3,472

Source: World Bank, *Debt Tables* (1983).

was carried out by governments, however, the most notable increases were in public external indebtedness (see Table 9.5); by the end of the decade, the 'debt problem' was already acute in Costa Rica, Honduras and Nicaragua; in El Salvador and Guatemala, the debt also grew rapidly after 1973, but started from a lower base.

At the end of the 1970s, therefore, the real economy in Central America had shown substantial progress,[17] but the financial side was looking dangerously exposed. Exchange-rate stability was no longer assumed in Costa Rica, where official devaluation had been adopted in 1974, nor in Nicaragua, where the Somoza administration had devalued shortly before its collapse; inflation had become a permanent reality, although the mechanisms for avoiding sharp changes in income distribution had not yet been developed; finally, a high level of foreign borrowing had avoided the need for recessionary policies, which in other circumstances would have had to be adopted to deal with both the deterioration in the net barter terms of trade and the tendency of government expenditure to outstrip revenue in an inflationary environment.

The 1979 depression

As with its predecessor the 1929 depression, 'the 1979 depression' is a phrase covering a series of events spread over several years. Certain export prices started falling before 1979, others not until the 1980s, and the cumulative effect of these changes did not produce a decline in economic activity throughout the region until 1982, a decline which (except in Costa Rica and Nicaragua) continued throughout 1983.[18] Provided this is clearly understood, no great harm is done by referring to these events as the 1979 depression.

Coffee prices, which had soared as a result of the 1975 frost in Brazil, peaked in 1977 and fell sharply the following year. As coffee is a major source of export earnings for all five Central American republics,[19] this fall reversed the sharp rise in export unit values of the 1976/7 period; import unit values, however, continued to rise after 1977 and the net barter terms of trade throughout the region began to decline in 1978.

The deterioration in the terms of trade in 1978 accelerated in the following years as a result of two factors: the rise in import unit values and the fall in non-coffee export prices. The former reached double figures in 1979 and 1980,[20] while beef prices started to fall after 1979, sugar and cotton prices after 1980 and banana prices after 1981 (see Table 9.1).

The impact of these unfavourable export price movements on export earnings could not be reversed by increases in the quantum of exports as a consequence both of the world recession beginning in 1979 and of supply-side constraints. The latter were most apparent in war-torn Nicaragua, where export earnings peaked in 1978, and in post-Romero El Salvador, where the nationalization of the export trade and the first stage of the land reform programme had a predictable impact on traditional exports and export earnings after 1979. Elsewhere in the region, however, exports peaked in 1980 (see Table 9.6).[21]

As in the rest of Latin America, one consequence of ISI has been to change the structure of imports away from consumer goods towards intermediate and capital goods. In the case of Central America, this must be qualified by distinguishing between extra- and intra-regional imports, the latter still being dominated by consumer goods. Despite this, the import bill now consists mainly of goods which are complementary to domestic production, so that a decline in imports implies a decline in economic activity.

In order to avoid the fall in imports, with its predictable effect on output, incomes and employment, several republics tolerated a huge rise in their current-account deficits, financed in large part by a fall in net international reserves. In Guatemala, for example, the rise in imports in 1981 provoked a $565 million current-account deficit, while net capital inflows were only $288 million, and total international reserves collapsed from $445 million at the end of 1980 to $150 million at the end of 1981.

In Costa Rica and Honduras, the attempt to increase imports by value was abandoned after 1980, as the current-account deficit in that year

Table 9.6 *Central America: imports, exports and balance-of-payments current account (million dollars), 1977–83*

	77	78	79	80	81	82	83
Costa Rica							
Exports f.o.b.	828	864	942	1,001	1,003	871	851
Imports f.o.b.	925	1,049	1,257	1,375	1,090	780	894
Current account balance	−226	−364	−558	−663	−409	−198	−382
El Salvador							
Exports f.o.b.	974	802	1,132	1,075	798	704	732
Imports f.o.b.	861	951	955	897	898	826	880
Current account balance	+31	−286	+21	+31	−250	−152	−95
Guatemala							
Exports f.o.b.	1,160	1,092	1,222	1,520	1,299	1,200	1,092
Imports f.o.b.	1,087	1,284	1,402	1,473	1,540	1,284	1,056
Current account balance	−35	−271	−206	−163	−565	−375	−224
Honduras							
Exports f.o.b.	530	626	757	850	784	677	675
Imports f.o.b.	550	654	783	954	899	681	705
Current account balance	−129	−157	−192	−317	−393	−228	−213
Nicaragua							
Exports f.o.b.	637	646	616	450	500	408	428
Imports f.o.b.	704	553	389	803	922	724	778
Current account balance	−82	−25	+180	−379	−514	−469	−397

Sources: International Financial Statistics (October 1984), and Inter-American Development Bank, *Annual Report* (1984).

widened to unprecedented levels (see Table 9.6). In El Salvador, the decline in imports by value began as early as 1979 as a consequence of capital flight which dried up the supply of foreign exchange for imports of goods. In Nicaragua, imports by value reached their first peak in 1977, falling in 1978 and 1979 as a result of capital flight and the civil war. The recovery after the war was short-lived, however, and imports by value reached their second peak in 1981 when the current account deficit ($514 million) exceeded the value of exports f.o.b. ($500 million).

The efforts to increase the value of imports despite stagnant or declining export earnings was financed not only through falls in international reserves (see Table 9.7), but also through increases in foreign borrowing, and the public external debt climbed steadily throughout the early 1980s (see Table 9.5). By 1981, Costa Rica had defaulted on its external obligations and in 1983 Nicaragua again ran into difficulties with its creditors.[22] In 1983, Honduras was also unable to meet its commitments to its external creditors in full.

The external-payments strain experienced by Central America in the period 1979–81 financed an increase in the price of imports rather than their value. The real value of imports (see Table 9.8) had peaked by 1978 in Guatemala, El Salvador and Nicaragua and only in Honduras did their level increase significantly in 1979. By 1981, the volume of imports was falling in all republics except Nicaragua and by 1982 a dramatic decline was experienced everywhere.

The recent sharp fall in the real value of imports has been due to the austerity programmes carried out in each republic, in several cases as part of

Table 9.7 *Net change in official international reserves 1977–83 (million dollars)*
A minus sign indicates an increase.

	1977	1978	1979	1980	1981	1982	1983
Costa Rica	119.6	−27.3	119.8	−91.6	52.3	−118.1	59.1
El Salvador	−41.0	−55.5	133.9	74.6	48.9	−70.1	−179.0
Guatemala	−179.6	−72.7	25.5	256.7	303.6	34.9	−30.0
Honduras	−66.3	−9.4	−19.8	77.7	71.8	88.5	8.0
Nicaragua	−9.1	83.6	−5.0	196.6	−57.7	99.5	−70.5

Source: Inter-American Development Bank, *Annual Report* (1983), Table 55.

Table 9.8 *Central America: real value of imports of goods and services (millions of 1980 dollars)*

	1978	1979	1980	1981	1982	1983
Costa Rica	1,418	1,459	1,409	1,047	711	741
El Salvador	1,290	1,147	911	843	702	659
Guatemala	1,419	1,314	1,201	1,156	916	728
Honduras	865	925	971	851	588	549
Nicaragua	720	502	912	947	706	656

Source: Inter-American Development Bank, *Annual Report* (1983), Table 7, and *Annual Report* (1984), Table 7.

the conditions attached to IMF loans.[23] Exchange-rate stability was abandoned explicitly in Costa Rica after December 1980[24] and there have been *de facto* devaluations in El Salvador and Nicaragua.[25] In Honduras, tariff surcharges have reduced the demand for imports[26] and throughout the region non-price rationing has been applied to reduce the demand for foreign exchange.

The most notable feature of the austerity programmes, however, outside of Nicaragua, has been the restraint on the public sector. The contribution of the government sector to GDP in real terms has shown no increase since 1980[27] and the budget deficit as a proportion of GDP fell sharply in 1982 in Costa Rica and Guatemala (see Table 9.3), while even in El Salvador there was a modest decline.

The continued effect of the decline in export earnings, the restraint on the public sector and the fall in real imports was sufficient to provoke a fall in real GDP throughout the region in 1982. The decline had begun a year earlier in Costa Rica, and as early as 1979 in El Salvador, while Nicaragua had experienced two years of rapid decline in 1978–9 followed by two years of economic recovery (1980–1). By 1982, however, the whole region was in the grip of a severe depression which shows no immediate sign of ending. In the period 1980 to 1983, real GDP per head had fallen by some 25 per cent in El Salvador, some 20 per cent in Costa Rica and nearly 15 per cent in Guatemala and Honduras.

The recent decline in GDP has been disproportionately concentrated in those sectors dependent on imports for their survival, in particular manufacturing, construction and commerce. The latter, which has traditionally earned a high share of its income from the resale of imported consumer goods, has been very severely hit by import restraint; in Costa Rica, for example, its share of GDP fell from 18 per cent in 1980 to 13.5 per cent in 1982.

Manufacturing production has been affected not only by the shortage of complementary imports, but also by the shrinking of the regional market. The value of CACM trade declined sharply after 1980,[28] as regional tensions led to a closing of borders and the scarcity of foreign exchange produced a series of beggar-my-neighbour policies designed to produce an export surplus with CACM partners. Paradoxically, those countries which have realized a surplus on trade within CACM have seen their advantage eroded as payment has often been blocked.

A further problem affecting manufacturing output, as well as several other sectors, has been the shrinking of the domestic market not only through the fall in mean real income, but also through a deterioration in the

Table 9.9 *Central America: real wages, 1979–82 (index numbers)*

	Base year	1979	1980	1981	1982
Costa Rica[a]	1975	140.5	136.5	121.2	92.6
El Salvador[b]	1970	88.3	82.9	72.2	64.6
Guatemala[a]	1970	68.6	62.0	66.7	65.2
Honduras	1976	102.0	96.0	104.0	104.0
Nicaragua	1975	95.9	81.7	79.7	69.8

[a] Based on wage data held by social security institute.
[b] Agricultural labourers only.
Source: Inforpress, *Centroamericana* (June 1983), no. 548, p. 10.

distribution of income. Real wages (see Table 9.9) have fallen sharply in Costa Rica, El Salvador and even Nicaragua since 1979, while their level in Guatemala is far below that recorded in 1970.

The agricultural sector has been subject to two contradictory forces in the recent period, as so often in the past. While export agriculture (EXA) has tended to shrink in real as well as money terms, agriculture for the home market – domestic-use agriculture (DUA) – has been able to benefit from the restrictions on imports[29] and deliberate government policies. The two effects have tended to cancel each other out in Costa Rica, Guatemala and Honduras, while the decline in EXA has been dominant in El Salvador (producing an overall fall in agricultural net output) and the rise in DUA has been dominant in Nicaragua (producing an overall rise in agricultural net output since 1982).

The 1979 depression has therefore not fallen with equal severity on all sectors; while real net output in agriculture has tended to stagnate, increasing the sector's share of real GDP, value added by industry, commerce and construction has fallen quite sharply.[30] Changes within the agricultural sector, however, have been of importance and the rural economy has not been spared the dramatic fall in real income per person which has afflicted the urban economy.

The 1929 depression and the mechanisms of recovery

As with the 1979 depression, the '1929 depression' is a phrase covering the decline in economic activity over a period of years, which began in Costa Rica as early as 1927, but which did not affect Honduras until the fiscal year 1931/2.[31]

The 1929 depression in Central America was brought on by a collapse of export earnings. With exports dominated by earnings from coffee and bananas,[32] the sharp fall in the price of the former and the volume of the latter[33] provoked a collapse in foreign-exchange receipts to about one-quarter of the pre-depression peak. For a brief period, an attempt was made to sustain the level of imports, but the difficulty of securing a net capital inflow from abroad and the requirements of public external debt-servicing forced each republic to run a trade surplus during the worst years of the depression (1930–2) and the value of imports collapsed even more rapidly than exports.

The decline in the value of external trade provoked a fiscal crisis through its impact on trade taxes and government revenue. Efforts to cut back government expenditure, consisting mainly of wages and salaries, contributed to the political crisis in 1930 and 1931 and were not wholly successful; public-sector deficits then had to be financed through increases in the internal debt.[34]

The public-sector deficits were not the result of Keynesian demand management (although a half-hearted attempt at a public works programme was made in Costa Rica)[35] and government expenditure in money terms declined.[36] With private consumption and investment (both private and public) adversely affected by the fall in imports, all items of expenditure moved pro-cyclically with exports, and the money value of GDP declined dramatically.[37]

Expressed in money terms, there is clearly no comparison between the 1929 and 1979 depressions. The former was much more severe and the collapse of export prices (particularly coffee and sugar) has no parallel with today. In real terms, however, the parallels are much closer: the volume of traditional exports kept up surprisingly well in the worst years of the depression and, although the net barter terms of trade of coffee producers deteriorated,[38] import prices also fell quite sharply.

Thus, the decline in real GDP and real GDP per head (see Table. 9.10) bears comparison with the falls in recent years. Indeed, the collapse of economic activity in El Salvador since 1979 and in Nicaragua between 1978 and 1979 is much more severe than during the 1929 depression.

Furthermore, the dominant role played by external factors in both depressions is readily apparent. In both cases, the depression was triggered off by unfavourable commodity-price movements; in the 1929 depression this leads to a collapse of export earnings, while in the 1979 depression it leads to a stagnation of earnings; since the latter depression, however, is taking place against a background of rising rather than falling world prices,

Table 9.10 *Central America: annual average rates of change of GDP and GDP per head, 1929–39 (%)*

Figures in parentheses refer to GDP per head.

	1929–34	1934–9
Costa Rica	0.2 (−2.1)	8.0 (5.5)
El Salvador	−0.7 (−2.1)	3.3 (2.0)
Guatemala	−0.6 (−3.2)	12.5 (10.3)
Honduras	−2.4 (−4.5)	0.2 (−2.6)
Nicaragua	−4.9 (−6.8)	2.4 (0.3)

Source: See Bulmer-Thomas, 1984, *op. cit.* (n. 11), Table 1.

the impact on real imports in both depressions is the same and their volume declines.

The fiscal crisis in the 1929 depression was provoked by the collapse of revenue from taxes on external trade. These have declined in importance in the intervening years, but some two-thirds of government revenue are still obtained from indirect taxes, which tend to move pro-cyclically with the value of external trade.

In both fiscal crises, however, an important role has been played by service payments on the external public debt. In the 1929 depression, fixed nominal payments in a period of falling prices together with currency depreciation (Costa Rica, El Salvador) pushed service payments to between 20 per cent and 30 per cent of government revenue. In the more recent crisis, fixed nominal payments would have been a blessing rather than a burden (because of inflation), but interest rates have been flexible upwards and currency depreciation has added to the problems in Nicaragua and Costa Rica.

In the 1929 depression, there were no international lending agencies to lay down conditions for borrowing. Nevertheless, the governments' hands were frequently tied either by the presence of a foreign controller of customs or by agreements with foreign bond-holders on the disposition of revenues. In both periods, an attempt was made to cut the public-sector deficit back to a level which could be financed without an increase in the internal debt, although in neither case was it very successful.

As Table 9.10 makes clear, the five-year period after 1934 was marked by rapid growth in several republics, Honduras being a notable exception. This recovery is all the more surprising, given that coffee prices remained close to their floor throughout the 1930s and that banana exports continued to be affected by disease in Honduras and Costa Rica.

The collapse of coffee prices after 1929 put at risk the leading export sector in all Central American republics outside Honduras. Property values fell and growers were threatened with foreclosure by their creditors (mainly commercial banks and exporters). Associations grew up to defend growers, and the authoritarian state, which after 1930 replaced its liberal, oligarchic predecessor,[39] intervened by declaring a debt moratorium and aiding coffee growers in several other ways.

State intervention made possible the continuance of the volume of coffee exports at pre-depression levels and this helped to prevent further falls in real GDP. It was not, however, a mechanism of recovery and the export sector did not play a dynamic role in the 1930s.

The dynamic role was provided essentially by import-substitution; this was not so much import-substitution in industry (ISI) as in agriculture (ISA). The development of export specialization in Central America in the half-century up to 1930 had led to the neglect of agriculture for domestic use (DUA) and food imports in 1929 represented some 20 per cent of the import bill. The shortage of foreign exchange throughout the 1930s contributed to the development of ISA, a development which was further assisted by an improvement in the distribution of income.[40]

Import-substitution of both types was aided by tariff increases and currency depreciation (in Costa Rica and El Salvador). Nevertheless, ISI played only a minor role because the almost complete absence of an industrial base in the 1920s meant that there was no spare capacity to take advantage of import restrictions. The development of new industrial capacity makes much use of both foreign exchange and credit, and neither were available in the 1930s.[41]

An additional recovery mechanism was provided by debt default. Central American republics, in common with most of Latin America, withdrew from the gold standard after 1931, and after 1932 defaulted on their external debt obligations.[42] This eased the fiscal crisis considerably and freed a substantial part of government revenue for deployment elsewhere.[43]

Lessons for the 1980s

At the time of writing (late 1984), Central America is still in the grip of an economic depression. In addition, regional tensions (particularly in El Salvador) have contributed to a fall in real income and these problems are unlikely to end as the world moves out of recession. Nevertheless, for all

143

the republics the problem of economic recovery is a pressing one and poses the question of whether any lessons can be drawn from the experience of the 1930s.

In the 1920s, the Central American import bill was dominated by consumer goods. Their suppression in the 1930s led to a fall in the living standards of the urban middle and upper classes, but *ceteris paribus* import restrictions had little impact on production outside of the unimportant non-food-processing industrial sector. That is why EXA was able to maintain its previous level of output and DUA to expand despite a fall in real imports.

In the 1980s, the industrial sector contributes some 20 per cent to GDP and is highly dependent on imports for machinery, raw materials and spare parts. Furthermore, EXA is now more mechanized and more import-intensive (fertilizers, insecticides, etc.) than in the 1930s, while even DUA in certain cases (e.g. rice) has become dependent on complementary imports.

Thus, all tradable activities exhibit import-dependence, and production is likely to be adversely affected by import restrictions. In addition, the scope for ISA is much less in the 1980s than in the 1930s, for three reasons: first, the share of food imports in the total import bill in 1979 was much less than in 1929, and secondly, movements in income distribution have been, if anything, in favour of greater inequality.[44] Thirdly, land is much scarcer and the expansion of DUA no longer has a zero opportunity cost.[45]

Despite this, however, there are some signs that DUA might again contribute to recovery, albeit in a more modest way. Although it exhibits a certain import dependence, it is much less than that exhibited by other sectors so that shortage of foreign exchange is not so critical. Furthermore, land-reform programmes in El Salvador and Nicaragua have led to an increase in the relative importance of DUA, although in both cases this has occurred to some extent at the expense of an absolute decline in EXA.[46]

The problem of preventing a fall in the volume of traditional exports presents similar difficulties in the 1980s to the 1930s. In the 1930s, prices were falling faster than costs, while in the 1980s costs are rising with prices stable or falling; in both cases there has been a profit squeeze and coffee-growers in El Salvador, for example, in an echo of the 1930s, have called on the government to impose a debt moratorium.[47]

Through its control of export taxes, the exchange rate, import tariffs and credit, the state is in a powerful position to manipulate the net price received by growers and there is ample evidence that this process is well under way.[48] As in the 1930s, however, this is unlikely to do more than stabilize the volume of traditional exports, as world market conditions will remain unfavourable for these crops.[49]

The third recovery mechanism from the 1930s (debt default) does not look so promising. In the 1980s Central America cannot afford to run the risk of zero or negative capital inflows, because the cost of running a current-account surplus in terms of lost output would be very high. That is why all republics, even Nicaragua, are anxious to reschedule their external obligations rather than default unilaterally.

Rescheduling, however, as Nicaragua has found since 1981, does not represent a panacea. Indeed, the burden of debt-servicing remains very high even after a successful rescheduling and puts a continuing squeeze both on non-debt government expenditure and on merchandise imports. This reduces the degrees of freedom of Central American governments in the 1980s compared with the 1930s and it must be remembered that for several years to come a large share of any fresh capital inflow will be required simply to refinance the external debt.

The choice of rescheduling rather than debt default makes impossible two other possible recovery mechanisms, neither of which was attempted in the 1930s; the first is Keynesian demand management based on deficit financing, while the second is ISI in intermediate and capital goods. The first mechanism has never made much sense in the context of small, developing countries and is in any case ruled out by the conditions attached to loans contracted with the IMF (a pre-condition for loans from other sources).[50] The second mechanism is very import-intensive and is therefore ruled out by the squeeze on imports which can be expected to continue for some years to come. Furthermore, ISI in non-consumer goods is possible only at the regional level, which presupposes a degree of regional harmony totally lacking at present.

Conclusions

The above study of recovery mechanisms in the 1930s suggests that, if repeated in the 1980s, they would produce only a modest improvement in economic performance. This is true, despite the many parallels which exist between the 1929 and 1979 depressions.

The reasons why the old recovery mechanisms are no longer sufficient are related to changes in the structure of the economy in the intervening period. First, the composition of the import bill has changed in such a way that the level of home output is now much more sensitive to an import squeeze. There are no longer branches of the economy where production does not

145

require complementary imports. Within DUA, there are some crops which are not particularly import-intensive (e.g. maize), but land is no longer costlessly available for their expansion.

Secondly, the 1979 depression is taking place against a background of rising rather than falling prices. With money-wage rigidity apparent in both periods, the consequence was an improvement in income distribution in the 1930s, but probably a deterioration in income distribution in the 1980s. Thus, the market demand for many consumer goods in the 1980s has exhibited a further contraction in addition to that implied by the fall in mean real income.

The prospects for the 1980s therefore look more gloomy than the outcome of the 1930s and it is worth considering whether alternative recovery mechanisms may be available. After peaking in the late 1920s, Central America's net barter terms of trade went through a period of secular decline until the late 1940s. If this decline was reversed more rapidly after the 1979 depression, then clearly the foreign-exchange constraint would be eased. Import-intensive activities could then expand and the recovery would be on its way.

It is difficult to predict the course of commodity prices, but the prospects for Central America's traditional exports do not look particularly bright. Alone of the region's republics, Honduras in the 1930s had to wait on an improvement in the fortunes of export agriculture before a weak recovery could get under way. It seems equally probable that in the 1980s only a modest improvement can be expected from a change in the fortunes of EXA on its own.

Another possibility is that the production of manufactured goods for export outside the region may increase. Certainly, there is spare capacity in the many duty-free export-processing zones throughout the region and market opportunities have increased since the passing by the United States Congress of the Caribbean Basin Initiative. However, these exports are starting from a very low base and would have to grow very rapidly to make much impact on the growth of real GDP, even if they can overcome the formidable obstacles presented by the shortage of investment, skilled labour and management expertise.

It is not inconceivable that the foreign-exchange constraint, the principal barrier to growth at present throughout the region, will be lifted as a result of international initiatives through a mini-Marshall Plan for the region.[51] Over the last few years, several voices have been raised to this effect; without US support, however, such an initiative will not operate and at present neither the US Congress nor the Administration appears well disposed towards a massive injection of economic aid to the region.

We must conclude, therefore, that the prospects for economic recovery in the 1980s and for a resumption of rapid growth are poor. This prognostication could change if regional harmony were restored and economic cooperation resumed at the regional level; this, however, is a political question involving not just the Central American republics and, when the international dimension is introduced, the prospects are indeed more gloomy than they were fifty years ago.

NOTES

1 The title of this chapter was chosen before coming across an article by Carlos Díaz Alejandro comparing Latin America in the 1930s with the 1980s. Díaz Alejandro's article, however, does not in general draw on the Central American experience. See C. Díaz Alejandro, 'Stories of the 1930s for the 1980s', in P. Aspe Armella, R. Dornbush, and M. Obstfeld (eds.), *Financial Policies and the World Capital Market: The Problem of Latin American Countries* (Chicago, 1983).

2 Two recent exceptions are R. Feinberg and R. Pastor, 'Far from Hopeless: An Economic Program for Post-War Central America', in R. Leiken (ed.), *Central America: Anatomy of Conflict* (New York, 1984), and John Weeks, *The Economies of Central America* (New York, 1984), particularly Chapter 8.

3 In both 1929 to 1931 and 1979 to 1981, Honduras enjoyed positive, if modest, growth of real GDP. From 1979 to 1981, there was positive growth in Guatemala, and real GDP increased in Nicaragua in 1980, 1981 and 1983. These are the exceptions, however, and after both 1929 and 1979 falls in real GDP were common throughout Central America.

4 Some readers may object to the use of the singular 'economy' rather than the plural 'economies'. There are, of course, many important differences between the economies of the Central American republics and, where these are relevant, I shall use the plural form. Nevertheless, the region's economic performance over the long run can be analysed in terms of a model common to all republics and this similarity can be captured by the use of the singular form.

5 One way in which the openness of the economy can be expressed is through the ratio of exports to GDP. In 1979, for example, which comes close to the last 'normal' year, exports were just over 35 per cent of GDP in El Salvador, Honduras and Nicaragua, were 27 per cent in Costa Rica and 21 per cent in Guatemala. For middle-income countries as a whole, the percentage was 18%, a figure which is easily surpassed by all Central American republics except Guatemala even when extra-regional exports alone are considered.

6 See V. Bulmer-Thomas, 'Central America in the Inter-War Years' in R. Thorp (ed.), *Latin America in the 1930s* (London, 1984).

7 In the 1920s, 'traditional' exports refer to coffee and bananas only. By the 1970s, the list had been expanded to include cotton, sugar and beef.

8 Examples are provided by cardamom from Guatemala, clothing from El Salvador, timber from Honduras and light manufactures from Costa Rica.

9 In Honduras, hurricane damage in 1974 contributed to a fall in real GDP in 1974 and 1975, but this was independent of the oil crisis.

10 Estimates of the net barter terms of trade for each republic up to 1982 can be found in Figure 1 of V. Bulmer-Thomas, 'Economic Development Over the Long Run – Central America Since 1920', *Journal of Latin American Studies*, 15 (November 1983).

11 See V. Bulmer-Thomas, 'A Model of Inflation for Central America', *Bulletin of the Oxford University Institute of Economics and Statistics*, 39 (1977), pp. 319–32.

12 Between 1950 and 1970, the annual average rate of change of prices was below 1 per cent in Guatemala, below 2 per cent in El Salvador and Honduras and 2.1 per cent in Costa Rica. Figures are not available for the whole period for Nicaragua, but there is no reason to believe that the inflation rate was not in the same range.

13 Although at first there was a movement in this direction. See G. Siri and L. R. Domínguez, 'Central American Accommodation to External Disruptions', in W. Cline (ed.), *World Inflation and the Developing Countries* (Washington, D.C., 1981).

14 The coffee boom was sparked off by severe frost in Brazil in 1975.

15 In Costa Rica, for example, the yield from the coffee tax rose from 79.4 million colones in 1975 to 257.4 million colones in 1977.

16 In 1976, capital expenditure by central government rose by 66 per cent in El Salvador, 92 per cent in Costa Rica, and 151 per cent in Guatemala. See Inforpress, *Centroamericana 1982* (Guatemala, 1982).

17 Except in Nicaragua, where rapid growth up to 1977 was reversed in 1978 and 1979 as a consequence of the civil war.

18 In the reports prepared by each government in consultation with the Inter-American Development Bank for presentation to the EEC in September 1983, all countries predicted either a fall or zero growth in real GDP for 1983. Nicaragua, however, finally achieved a 5.3 per cent, and Costa Rica a 0.8 per cent, increase in real GDP.

19 The share of coffee earnings in total exports in 1978 was as follows: Costa Rica 43.5 per cent, El Salvador 51.9 per cent, Guatemala 43.5 per cent, Honduras 33.0 per cent and Nicaragua 30.8 per cent.

20 Except for 1979 in Honduras, where the rate of increase was 7 per cent. Figures are not given for Nicaragua, but are assumed to be in the same range (see Inforpress, *op. cit.*).

21 Export earnings in Costa Rica peaked in 1981, but the level was virtually the same as 1980.

22 The Nicaraguan external debt was renegotiated successfully in December 1980. Despite this, debt-servicing rose to 40 per cent of exports in 1982, forcing the government to seek a further accommodation with its creditors in 1983.

23 In addition to the compensatory financing facility, which comes without conditions when export earnings fall below trend, all Central American coun-

tries other than Nicaragua have received IMF loans subject to various conditions on domestic economic policies. The cornerstone of these conditions has been restraint on the public sector.

24 The collapse of the Costa Rican exchange rate has been dramatic since December 1980. While the official rate fell from 8.60 colones to 20 colones to the US dollar, the inter-bank rate has fallen to 44 colones and the free-market rate touched 80 colones to the dollar at one point. Virtually all merchandise trade is conducted at the inter-bank rate.

25 In Nicaragua, although the official exchange rate remains at 10 córdobas to the US dollar (unchanged since 1979) the exchange rate in the parallel market (through which much merchandise trade passes) is 28 córdobas, while the black market rate in October 1984 was 250 córdobas. In El Salvador, the official rate of 2.5 colones to the US dollar has not been changed since 1934, but the parallel market exchange rate in October 1984 was 4 colones. Some 80 per cent of trade was conducted at the official exchange rate in 1982, but this proportion declined sharply in 1983.

26 An additional 'temporary' tax of 20 per cent was imposed on all imported goods in 1982.

27 Except in Nicaragua, where value added by public administration rose by 12.6 per cent in real terms between 1980 and 1982.

28 Intra-regional exports in 1980 were valued at $1,129 million. These fell to $947 million in 1981 and $775 million in 1982.

29 Food imports at the beginning of the 1979 depression accounted for some 5 to 10 per cent of the import bill.

30 For the region as a whole, GDP at 1980 prices has fallen from $19,689 million in 1978 to $18,924 in 1982. During the same period, manufacturing value added fell from $3,680 to $3,386 million, net output in construction fell from $773 to $630 million and value added in commerce was reduced from $4,463 to $3,967 million. In the same period, agricultural value added fell by only 2.6 per cent to $4,719 million. See Inter-American Development Bank, *Regional Report for Central America* (September 1983), p. 30.

31 Official estimates for real GDP in the inter-war years are available only for Honduras. For the other republics, I have used my own estimates of the national accounts back to 1920 (see V. Bulmer-Thomas, 1984, *op. cit.*). The timing of the onset of the depression in both Costa Rica and Honduras was affected primarily by the spread of disease on the banana plantations.

32 In 1929, coffee and bananas accounted for some 90 per cent of exports from Costa Rica, El Salvador (coffee only) and Guatemala. In Nicaragua and Honduras, the export of precious metals pushed the figure for coffee and bananas down to 73 per cent and 87 per cent respectively.

33 After 1929, the banana trade was dominated by two multinational fruit companies, United Fruit and Standard Fruit. By cutting back on global production, they were able to avoid a sharp fall in banana prices in consuming countries; the impact of the depression in Central America was therefore experienced through reductions in banana volumes rather than prices, the exact opposite of coffee exports.

34 The internal debt rose sharply in all republics, except Nicaragua where

149

government finances were directly controlled by US officials under the Financial Plan of 1917. See I. J. Cox, *Nicaragua and the United States* (Boston, Mass., 1927).

35 See T. Soley Güell, *Compendio de Historia Económica y Hacendaria de Costa Rica* (San José, Costa Rica, 1975), pp. 100–8.

36 See League of Nations, *Public Finance, 1928–1935* (Geneva, 1937).

37 There are official estimates for money GDP (i.e. at current prices) for both Guatemala and Honduras. In the former case, nominal GDP is estimated to have fallen to one-quarter of its peak level (see Banco Central de Guatemala, *Memoria* (Guatemala, 1955)).

38 I have constructed the net barter terms of trade separately for the case of a country obtaining all its exports from coffee (the 'coffee terms of trade') or from bananas (the 'banana terms of trade'); see V. Bulmer-Thomas, 1984, *op. cit.*, Figure 2. For the more conventional country terms of trade in this period see V. Bulmer-Thomas, 1983, *op. cit.*, Figure 1).

39 Not all scholars of Central America would explain the political changes in these terms, but there is general agreement that the period marks a change in the dominant political model. See, in particular, E. Torres Rivas, *Interpretación del Desarrollo Social Centroamericano* (San José, Costa Rica, 1973).

40 The question of an improvement in income distribution during a period when governments were avowedly 'anti-labour' is a controversial one, although it is the only one consistent with the statistical evidence; see V. Bulmer-Thomas, 1984, *op. cit.*.

41 Before 1929, expansion of industry had relied either on self-finance or immigrant capital. An examination of bank balance sheets in the inter-war years suggests that credit for industry was virtually zero, in sharp contrast to the case of export agriculture (particularly coffee).

42 Honduras defaulted on her internal debt obligations only, however, honouring her external debt payments.

43 Between 1932 and 1934, external debt service in Costa Rica, for example, fell from 30 per cent to 12 per cent of government revenue.

44 Real wages have fallen (risen) faster (slower) than real GDP. This suggests a deterioration in the functional distribution of income; figures are not available on movements in the size distribution of income.

45 A surplus of both labour and land is responsible for the argument that DUA had a zero opportunity cost in the 1930s (capital not being used in significant amounts in DUA's production). Elsewhere, however, I have argued that even in the 1930s there were important differences in the availability of land between 'coffee republics' (El Salvador, Costa Rica and Guatemala) and 'banana republics' (Nicaragua and Honduras). See V. Bulmer-Thomas, 1984, *op. cit.*.

46 My own estimates (see V. Bulmer-Thomas, 1983, *op. cit.*, Figure 3) suggest that there has indeed been a relative increase in DUA since 1978. This, however, is not strictly relevant; by definition, DUA is not yet a recovery mechanism (GDP is still falling) and a relative increase should not be confused with an absolute one.

47 See Inforpress, *Centroamericana*, 11 August 1983, no. 554, p. 10.

48 The multinational fruit companies, for example, pressured the Honduran government into reducing the banana export tax in 1983.

49 Trade prospects for traditional exports over the medium term are considered in V. Bulmer-Thomas, 'Regional Integration, Trade Diversification and the World Market', in G. Irvin and X. Gorostiaga (eds.), *Towards an Alternative for Central America and the Caribbean* (forthcoming).

50 IMF conditionality does not apply to Nicaragua, which has no stand-by arrangement with the Fund. Keynesian demand-management techniques, however, remain as difficult to apply in Nicaragua as in the rest of Central America.

51 The Bipartisan Commission on Central America (the Kissinger Report) called for a massive injection of external finance between 1984 and 1990. Of the total of $20.6 billion (excluding Nicaragua), some $8.5 billion was to be provided by the US Government. Congress, however, has shown little support for voting such sums of money.

10 Conclusion

ESPERANZA DURÁN

It has been two years since the Latin American debt crisis erupted. Yet the prospects for the ability of the Latin American countries to pay interest on the debt, not to mention the repayment of the principal, look bleaker than when the crisis first started. There is a growing realization amongst debtors and creditors alike that what they face is not just a short-term liquidity problem but a 'structural imbalance'. This could be partly attributed to the outdated models of economic development that have prevailed in many debtor countries, but has been aggravated by the evolution of the international economic and financial system.

The world recession, which was the external factor contributing to the build-up of the crisis, has left a trail of negative consequences – high and rising interest rates, a decline in commodity prices, a wave of protectionism in the developed countries, to mention only the most important – which will hinder the capacity of the debtor countries to recover. Even if the debtors could check their course by efficient management of the domestic system of production and proceed along a healthy path of realistic exchange and interest rates, the constraints imposed on them by the external economic environment would be insurmountable.

The debt problem of the Third World in general, and Latin America in particular, has outgrown its own immediate limits and become one of global concern. Its economic, financial and consequent political repercussions have transcended the sphere of debtors and directly involved lenders (creditor banks and international financial institutions), becoming increasingly important to the governments of the industrialized world. It is now evident that the debt problem of the LDCs is closely interwoven with the future of the world economy, and that world economic recovery and the management of the debt crisis are closely linked.

The link between the economics and the politics of the Latin American debt crisis is a fascinating subject. In his contribution to this book, David

152

Stephen addresses himself to this dimension, seeking to assess the impact of the crisis and the world recession on the political nature or orientation of several Latin American regimes. He argues that a poor economic performance by a democratic government does not necessarily lead to its replacement by a military dictatorship. Looking at some countries could lead to inaccurate generalizations. Amongst the most notable of such examples is the case of Chile, where the democratically elected regime of Allende was toppled by the military following the economic chaos that resulted from the socialist experiment. But no such correlation between economic crisis leading to dictatorship can be established. Two striking cases in point are Argentina and Nigeria: in the former the debt crisis was one of the factors contributing to the demise of the military; in the latter the economic and debt crisis paved the way for a military take-over. Perhaps it is only *change* as such that follows from times of crisis?

It should also be noted that, as Stephen points out, military regimes differ very considerably in Latin America, and can indeed occupy different ends of the political spectrum: a progressive post-1968 military junta, with a large measure of state interventionism, or a neo-liberal free-market economy under General Pinochet. In this respect Latin America provided a good opportunity to examine the connection between the ideologies of the political regimes and their economic performance, given the considerable variety of styles and orientations of government the region has had. Stephen concludes that regardless of political ideology, the Latin American military chose to follow conservative economic policies and willingly lent themselves as vehicles for the recycling of petrodollars. From the point of view of the Western bankers the military regimes of South America seemed to provide the advantages that populist democracies (like those of Allende in Chile, Belaúnde in Peru, or the Argentine Peronist regime) could not provide: discipline, hard work and effective management of the economy, free from popular constraints inherent in a democracy *a la latinoamericana*. The debt crisis would not seem to attest to the bankers' sound political judgement.

The chapter by Jonathan Hakim deals with the domestic and international economic factors which led to the crisis. It is particularly rewarding to examine carefully the external economic environment. As Hakim explains, the recycling of petrodollars from the first oil shock proceeded smoothly. This was due to the fact that loans (as well as deposits in international banks) were short-term, and interest rates were low. In fact, taking into account world inflation, interest rates were often negative in real terms. It was as a result of the oil glut, and of the industrialized countries' fight against inflation through restrictive monetary policies, that interest rates reached unprecedented heights, dealing a heavy blow to the LDCs which had contracted debts with private banks at short term and with floating rates of interest. Prior to the crisis, banks were prepared to facilitate short-term loans, regarding them as carrying a low risk. However, the banks' miscalculation and excessive short-term lending had serious consequences which became evident when the Latin American countries, starting with Mexico, found and declared themselves unable to cope with debt-servicing.

In the context of domestic economic strategies the Latin American countries originally adopted, back in the 1950s, similar development models. These consisted of expansionary economic programmes, set in an unambiguous import-substitution framework, which seemed appropriate for countries with incipient industrialization and potentially large markets. Nevertheless, by the middle of the 1960s, economic policies in Latin America began to diverge and each country followed its own course, as illustrated by John Williamson's comparison of four Latin American countries – and by each of the case studies in the second part of this volume, namely Brazil, Mexico, Chile, Venezuela, and Central America. From pronounced forms of state interventionism in the economy, to the free-market monetarist experiments, Latin American economic models prevailing during the last two decades or so could hardly differ more. And yet, a debt crisis with similar features violently overtook much of the region in 1982. To be sure, apparent differences can be deceptive, and it becomes necessary to search for common denominators. Despite the differences in economic philosophies and models, there were similar errors of planning and management, alongside other characteristics in common, in countries with acute debt problems. Examples of these are:

   overvalued exchange rates, which made borrowing cheap, imports cheap and, in the event, stimulated the flight of capital;
   borrowing at short-term and floating exchange rates of interest to finance trade deficits and long-term development projects, without giving due regard to possible continuing rises in these rates beyond levels previously experienced;
   widespread corruption;
   and postponement of adjustments to world recession by not establishing early austerity measures, in line with international developments, and continuing expansionary policies through foreign borrowing.

The natural, compelling question here is, why was economic management so similar in many important regards, in countries with different economic conditions and endowments, and with markedly different systems and orientations of government?

Part of the answer can be found in their common drive for sustained expansion, even if having to mortgage the country, as was mentioned above in the context of Hakim's contribution. But this is surely not enough, as, for example, the Asian NICs underwent a similar process of sustained heavy borrowing to finance expansion, and yet have weathered the storm rather successfully.

It seems clear that a second major element in trying to answer the question lies in the nature of the Latin American import-substitution model and its preservation past a certain stage of industrialization when its drawbacks came to dominate. The comparison of the development strategies of the Asian and Latin American NICs by Gustav Ranis and Louise Orrock is relevant here. The corollary is that the export-led development pattern of the former, facilitated by their unique socio-political conditions, fared better in the context of the world recession, by making their ratio of export to debt-servicing manageable, on the macroeconomic side, and by placing them on a much stronger footing in the increasingly competitive world markets as far as production structure and efficiency is concerned.

The debt crisis was prompted as much by internal as by external factors. The solution, therefore, must of necessity lie on both fronts.

There is agreement that the debt burden of the LDCs must be firmly tackled by all sides involved, and that reasonable solutions must urgently be found and implemented; indeed, one can already see greater involvement on the part of the governments of the industrial countries with the private banks.

Several lines of action have been proposed, although no consensus seems to exist as to what measures – or combination of measures – should be taken: there is discussion of interest-rate capping; capitalizing of interest rates; 'multi-year' rescheduling of official and commercial debts; and increased contributions to institutions such as the IMF and the World Bank. But banks seem reluctant to decide on the adoption of the first three, and the industrial governments seem to shy away from the last, which would in effect amount to the transfer of part of the debt burden of the LDCs onto the taxpayers of the developed countries.

Whatever overall solution to the debt crisis is eventually reached, for the moment only partial solutions are in sight: concessions that creditors have been forced to make here and there; and mainly, at the domestic level, the implementation of short-term austerity programmes in the debtor countries. There is widespread consensus, however, that these IMF 'packages' are unsustainable in the medium and long term, both economically and politically.

On the other hand, the scale and multiplication of rescheduling agreements with, and proposals by, Latin American countries, under the guidelines of the IMF austerity programmes, may well ease the short-term liquidity problem. But these measures are only pushing the problem into the future, when durable solutions may well be yet more difficult. New rises in interest rates and continued budget deficits in the United States make the future of the world economy look uncertain, and certainly that of the big LDC debtors.

Real solutions have to be found, and these need to come from three fronts. First, international trade and investment should lead the way out of the recession by a mixture of less restrictive monetary and financial policies in the United States and elsewhere and a reversal of recent protectionist trends. Secondly, at the level of international finance, major one-off concessions are imperative – either interest-rate capping or any of its variants mentioned above, and/or increased financial assistance by governments of the developed countries through the international financial institutions. Lastly, a major change is required in the development strategies of the Latin American economies. A modicum of austerity needs to be preserved and sustained. But a major second line of action is necessary and the debt shock seems to be having the salutary effect of forcing the Latin American countries to realize it. Namely, a sound long-term development model will have to do away with inefficient production structures, with a system of utterly distorted prices and highly subsidized public sectors and services, of unrealistic exchange and interest rate policies, all of which have resulted in a persistent inability to earn, through exports or investment, the foreign currency that their development process requires.

Index

Index

Singapore, 49; exports, 52, 53; growth rate, 55

Somoza García, Anastasio, 135

South Korea: agricultural sector, 49, 50, 52, 54, 56, 57, 65; growth rate, 51, 54, 55, 62; import- and export-substitution, 50, 51, 54; income distribution, 54, 55, 56–7; industrial exports, 24, 51, 53; level of protectionism, 54, 60; mineral exports, 50, 52; similarities with Latin American NICs, 65

Soviet bloc relations with Latin American countries, 3, 4, 7, 9, 10

stabilization programmes, 28, 38, 39, 40, 43, 48

structural problems of Latin American economies, 24–6, 84–6, 91, 152

sugar prices, 131, 132, 136, 141

Taiwan: agricultural sector, 49–50, 52, 54, 56, 57; exports, 51, 52, 53; growth rate, 51, 54, 55; import- and export-substitution, 50–2, 54; income distribution, 54, 55, 56, 57, 61; protectionism, 54

tariffs, trade barriers, Latin American, 22, 24, 39, 131; reduction of, 42, 43, 105, 110

Tello, Carlos, 82

terms of trade, 76, 117, 132, 136

trade-cycle model, 130

trade liberalization, 42, 43, 45, 65, 98, 105

trade union(s), 11, 90; bureaucracy, 3; corruption, 5; power, 63, 64

Tupumaros, 10

unemployment, 49, 61, 63

United States, 27, 37, 62, 75, 77, 116; bank loans to Latin America, 23, 35, 73; and Central America, 146–7; economy, 20, 21, 34, 36, 83, 156; Federal Reserve Board, 23; and Mexico, 23, 85, 86–7; political and economic relations with Latin America, 8, 10, 11, 12, 73, 75, 77, 124, 149 n. 34.

urbanization, 11, 128, 131

Uruguay, 9, 10, 23, 46; military coup, 2, 3, 4

Vargas, Getúlio, 75

Velasco Alvarado, Juan, 2, 10

Venezuela, 18, 24, 120–9, 154; agrarian reform and agriculture, 127–8; Central Bank, 122, 123, 126; corruption, 126–7; democracy, 120, 126, 129; external debt, debt crisis, 19, 23, 26, 29, 33, 122–3, 125–7, 128–9; foreign policy, 121, 123–5; and IMF, 124, 127, 128–9; import-substituting industrialization, 127; nationalization of oil industry, 121–2, 124; oil boom, 120–3, 128; political aspect of debt, 126; political and economic history, 120; role in OPEC, 121, 123; Venezuelan Investment Fund loans, 124

Vial, Javier, 113

Videla, General Jorge, 2, 4, 10

Vuskovic, Pedro, 4

wage(s), 140; policy, 40, 42, 43, 63; rises, 54, 55; *see also* income distribution

Whitehead, Laurence, 90

World Bank, 18, 27, 37, 124, 155

world economic recession, 1, 21, 152, 155; and Central American depression, 130–47; impact on Latin American economies, 18, 48, 83, 87, 115, 127, 154; prospects for recovery, 152, 156